"I don't believe people are looking for the meaning of life as much as they are looking for the experience of being alive."

Joseph Campbell, Mythologist, writer, lecturer

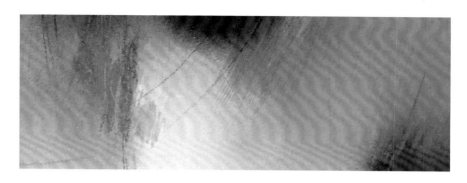

WHAT IS DEATH?
MESSAGES FROM THE HEART

LEXIE BROCKWAY POTAMKIN
Original Art from Paintings by Deborah Lieberman Fine

Editorial: • *Art Direction:* Elliott Curson • *Design:* Rhona Candeloro • *Editor:* Phil Beck

Library of Congress Cataloging-in Publication Data

What Is Death? Messages From The Heart / [compiled by] Lexie Brockway Potamkin; Artwork by Deborah Lieberman Fine.

ISBN 978-0-9824590-2-7 (Hardcover)

First Printing, October, 2011

Printed by Palace Press, China.

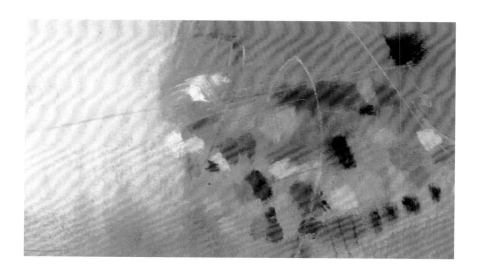

I dedicate this book to all of humanity. I honor the divinity in you and the divinity in me.

"For life and death are one, even as the river and the sea are one."

Kalil Gibran, *On Death*

ACKNOWLEDGMENTS

This book on death and life would not have been possible without the participation of hundreds of caring people who generously shared their own experiences, insights and thoughts about death. Thank you. Thank you. Thank you.

My friend Deborah Lieberman Fine has created the art in *What is Death*, filling the pages with beauty, joy, color, power and depth. If you look closely at her work, you will see it is multidimensional and heavenly. For me, her abstract, strong colors convey spirit, peace, love and the beauty of death.

A huge thank you to Elliott Curson, Laurie Sue Brockway, Tony Tognucci, Rhona Candeloro, Phil Beck, Karla Kuban and Juan Guerrero — an awesome team whose support, ideas, love and vision crafted this beautiful book.

Thank you to all my guides, teachers, angels, family and friends. Your love and support makes everything possible.

Contents

Forward by Steven E. Hodes, MD xi

Introduction xvii

What is Death? Responses From People of All Backgrounds . .1

How Different Religions and Classic Thinkers View Death . .122

Think About Your Legacy 134

Planning A Meaningful Funeral 138

Epilogue 140

About Lexie Brockway Potamkin .165

About Deborah Lieberman Fine 166

Final Thoughts 168

Inspirational Sources 174

Index 176

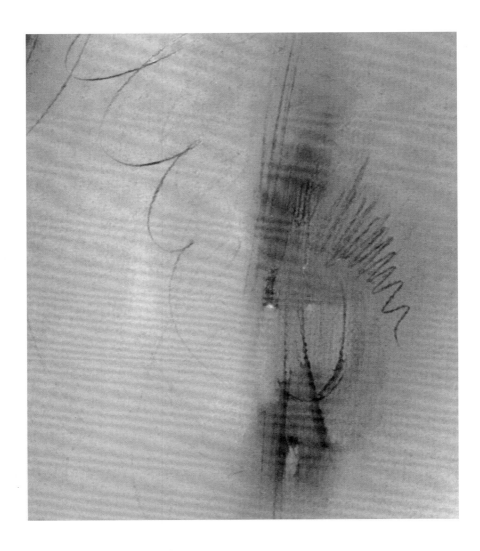

FORWARD

Death is One of Life's Most Compelling Mysteries

Since the dawn of human consciousness, no subject has affected our arts, science, philosophy, religion and dreams more then the realization that death — the cessation of life as we know it — is certain and unavoidable.

It is a topic that is feared, dreaded and misunderstood. In many ways, death is one of life's most compelling mysteries. Medically speaking, we know that death occurs when there is cessation of brain function, essentially a flat EEG tracing. However, on a spiritual level, there are a myriad of points of views about where the soul goes once the body is no longer viable.

It is for this reason that we should welcome Lexie Brockway Potamkin's book. It is a bold attempt to face and explore the subject that is so often denied and repressed. It reflects her personal confrontation with death and her journey to overcome the fear that infects us all. We can all be inspired by her courage to create a book that gives a platform for so many views on death, dying and the journey of the soul.

Physicians are trained to *prevent* people from dying and they are, unfortunately, poorly equipped to deal with death. To us, death represents defeat, a failure of some kind. We believe we should have done something different, diagnosed the patient sooner or offered better treatment.

Physicians are trained to believe that death is the end of existence. Yet there is a growing recognition in our culture, and among some medical professionals, that the physical body is a vehicle given to us for a certain amount of time. And that when we leave the body, the soul moves on to another realm of being. Many people also believe that loved ones continue to commune with us, and guide us, after death.

My own investigations in 35 years as a physician — including personal interviews with individuals who have had near-death experiences, after-death communications, medium and psychic interactions — have provided me with the evidence to conclude that physical death is not the end of existence.

From a medical and biologic perspective, life and death are inextricably intertwined. On a cellular level, cells are born, mature and die constantly. In fact, half a million cells die every second, 50 billion per day. The cells which comprise our skin, GI tract and immune system are constantly dying and being renewed. Death precedes life on a cellular basis. With this basic biologic truth,

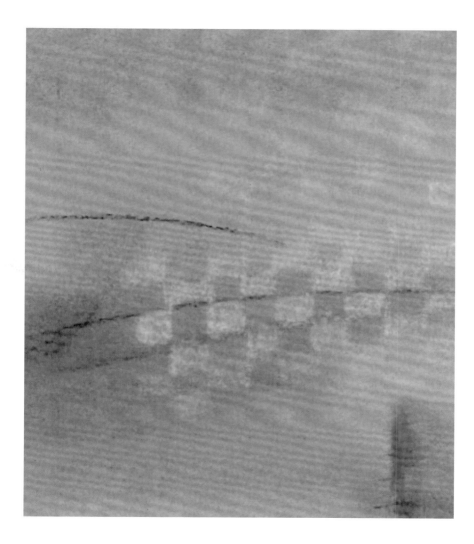

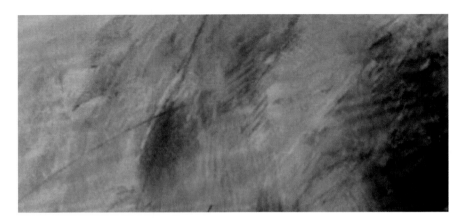

there is no option other than ultimate physical death.

Death frightens us on two deeply profound levels: the end of our personal existence and the fear of what awaits us, and the loss of our most deeply cherished loved ones.

If we could have some sense that death is not the ultimate end, we could more easily accept what we cannot change. Facing our fears allows us to make peace with them, to mindfully sit with them and accept their reality. The end of life, and going through the loss of loved ones, could be a time of grace.

From a medical perspective in which physical suffering is unrelenting and hopeless, death offers the ultimate end to such torment. Ironically, this is perhaps a form of healing — relief for the one who is suffering and for loved ones who struggle seeing someone they care for in such pain.

It is human nature to believe in the back of our minds that the people we love, and we ourselves, are immortal. When life brings death, it can be devastating.

Lexie Brockway Potamkin speaks to another form of immortality, that of the soul. Her prescription for facing and confronting the tragedy of death is simple but profound — through love.

In this book, she has sought the insights of others from a variety of disciplines and backgrounds. This offers the reader many perspectives to consider. They are unique to each contributor but share the underlying quest to make sense of the nature of death.

This approach leaves the final perspective to the reader. It is what makes this book an invaluable addition to the literature on the subject of death.

What is Death? offers an invitation to boldly explore the fate that awaits every living being. By being open and inquisitive, the reader will discover that death is not the enemy. In fact, it is not even the end. The real enemy is the fear to explore it.

Steven. E. Hodes, MD

Steven E. Hodes, MD is a board-certified physician with 35 years in private practice, based in Edison and Old Bridge, New Jersey. He has a degree in religious studies. In addition to his medical practice, he has devoted himself to speaking and writing about metaphysics and healing, with an eye toward helping people regain their health, strength and the ability to explore life's challenges from a more spiritual perspective. He is author of Meta-Physician on Call for Better Health: Metaphysics and Medicine for Mind, Body and Spirit.

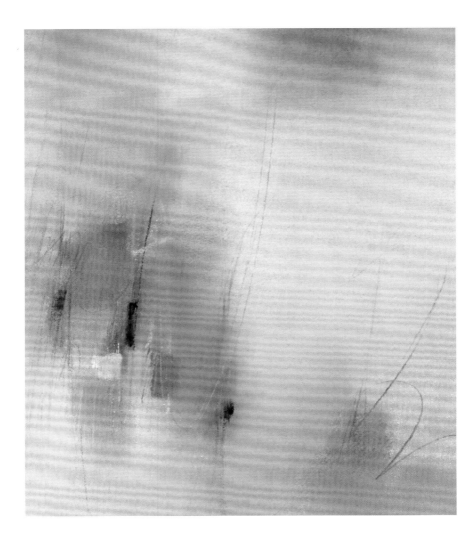

INTRODUCTION

After I finished writing *What is Love?* a tiny voice said to me, "Write *What is Death?*" Love and death are so intertwined and each teaches us about life.

A dear friend once said, "The three most important days of our lives are the day we are born, the day we figure out why we were born and the day we die." Our divine purposes are as varied as human beings are unique.

Perhaps one of the most important questions we can ask ourselves is: If I die tomorrow, how will I be remembered? Your answer will teach you how to live. Through this book I hope you can find more meaning in your life by better understanding and accepting our inevitable transition into the next realm.

Death has long been a taboo topic for people. We avoid it. We dance around it. We don't really know what to say when someone dies. We are taught to believe funerals are depressing and loss of life is a tragedy.

Death in our society is generally seen as a negative thing, rather than a continuation of a natural cycle that begins when we are born — intensifying as we become more emotionally and spiritually evolved — and comes to fruition when we die.

Death will always remain the great mystery. It is our personal faith that defines our feelings and thoughts about death. I believe that faith can grow as we open our hearts to gentleness, love and compassion. This openness prepares us for death and teaches us how to live today.

What is Death, Anyway?

What is death? That is a question that I began grappling with as a child — starting when I lost my first dear pet, and then when my beloved father died. He was so young. He lived with such compassion, forgiveness, love and grace. I wondered how God could take him, how someone so kind would be allowed to die and if I would ever see him again.

Since then, beloved pets, relatives, friends and, more recently, my wonderful mom have passed on. Just as I was there to see my first grandchild born into the world, I have been there to see people I love leave this place. Over time I have come to know, through my personal experiences, that death, like birth, is a natural, remarkable process.

Like so many people who shared their thoughts in this book, I learn more each day to peacefully accept death with the sense that it is not the end, the last stop or the "demise" of loved ones. To me it feels as if those I love have moved into another room, and that they are never truly far away. I miss them, but I am not without them.

The question "What is Death?" can be pondered on so many

levels: emotional, physical, spiritual, medical, metaphysical. Where do we go when we "cross over?" How does the soul move on? What happens in the last breath of life that takes us into death? Do our loved ones greet us on the other side?

In preparing this book, I interviewed hospice workers around the country who have pondered death's significance and value. Many reported their patients' recounting of near-death experiences. Perhaps you've heard a similar description: "It felt like my soul crossed over to a most profound, loving place, but this was not my time, so I had to stay on Earth."

Although accounts of these kinds of experiences are becoming more and more common, medicine and science have yet to validate them. But there are many small miracles that occur every day that defy logical, linear explanation.

One day a few months ago, I walked into my office and saw a vivid rainbow lighting up the room. I asked my assistant if he saw the same thing, and he said yes. He had worked in that space for several years, but had never seen such light. Consider that a rainbow is the result of sun shining through water drops in the air between you and the sun. The raindrops act as small prisms, separating the light into colors.

There was no direct sunlight in my office, and there could not have been water drops in the air. What was the explanation? I don't believe such a force to be nuclear, gravitational or electromagnetic — something described by science alone.

Every day science makes new discoveries regarding forces,

fields and particles. But I believe I was witness to another dimension. Perhaps scientific principles formed some basis for the rainbow's appearance; but I felt its presence as something extraordinary, something mystical. It's possible that all three — mystical forces along with science and religion — might have had something to do with my rainbow, but I can't explain it, and neither can anyone else.

I like to believe that my mother appeared to me as this rainbow; a reminder that she is still with me. When I take a moment to slow down and think of mom, I love the idea that our dear, departed loved ones continue to make themselves known to us earthly beings.

As Others See It

Every religion has its own beliefs and teachings: Christians believe in a heaven where they will be greeted by Jesus; Hindus believe the soul continues to reincarnate; Native Americans believe that the soul becomes part of nature; and atheists believe, basically, that "when you are dead, you're dead." There are thousands of spiritual schools of thought that give us even more ways to view dying, death and the fate of the soul.

Each person possesses his or her own view — sometimes shaped by religious beliefs, yet often enhanced by personal experience. Even the most devout of us may see beyond the veil of current religious understanding or logic when faced with illness, death or the trials of going through a death experience with a loved one. The death of someone close changes us forever, and often motivates us to search even deeper for answers.

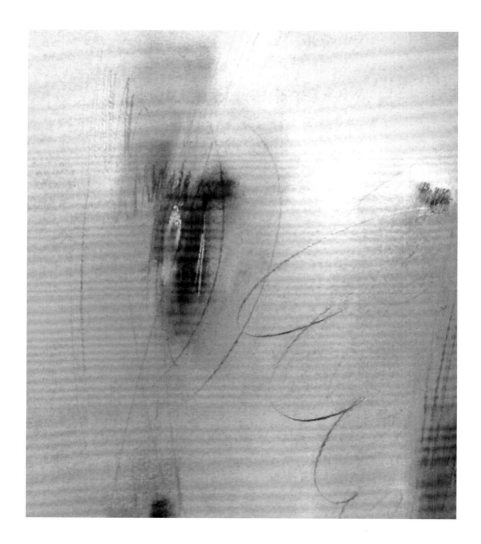

In this book you'll find theories, beliefs, personal wisdom, experience-based knowledge and intuitive insights from almost 150 people of various religious backgrounds, customs and beliefs. From doctors and clergy to people who rarely talk about death and dying, their diverse views point to so many possibilities. It is my hope that just by reading through their responses, new doors of understanding will open for you.

Loss Leads to Learning

As time goes on we begin to lose those close to us, but we learn much from those losses. I learned from my uncle. He was 97 years old, and lived with my family the last six months of his life. In his final weeks, he told me fascinating stories about his time on Earth — he was a bachelor until age 60, and divorced his wife at age 90. He told me his divorce was stressful, and he didn't want to re-marry. Each day, even when he was in a coma, I rolled him out into the sun. (He was a sun worshipper, and his leathered skin showed it.)

The day he died, I placed my hands on his shoulders and said, "Nat, I believe there are angels all around you. You are completely loved." He opened his eyes, smiled and gently let go. At that moment, I felt a deep, peaceful, calming kind of love that to this day I can hardly explain. It was more than anything a gift — an awakening to a better understanding of the calmness that can be found in death.

My first really big loss was my father when I was 19. My dad made such a huge impact on my life because of his honorable character. He lived the Ten Commandments and then some. When I think of dying with a full life behind me, I think of my dad's as an example. He died young, but lived with compassion, forgiveness, love and grace and that very fact gave me comfort when he passed; it made his loss less abrupt and gut-wrenching than I anticipated.

When my dear mother died not too long ago, my close friend Alvin remarked, "Death is so final." Death feels final to me most of the time. However, I experience moments of continuance. By that I mean I can still feel my mom's love and presence, especially in times of prayer and meditation. Somehow our relationship continues on a very subtle level.

My mom always told us that we are not supposed to look back, only look forward. I believe that is true in life and death. In life, we must look beyond the obvious, not have regrets and learn to let go. Upon death, we must look beyond, not back, and let go.

An hour before my mom crossed over, I whispered in her ear, "I love you, Mom. You are the best mom in the world. I feel completely loved by you, and your love for me will live in my heart forever. I'm so blessed and grateful that you are my mom. I love you, I love you, I love you. Thank you for being my wisdom teacher, my best friend and the best mom ever."

I rubbed frankincense, myrrh and lavender oils on her feet, hands and head. In my heart, I let her go, I did not cling to my roiling emotions — but felt love and gratitude. I asked friends, Tibetan monks of the Drepung Loseling Monastery, to pray and chant for my mom. After she passed, they visited her apartment, brought roses and performed some of the sacred funerary rites spelled out in the *Bardo Thodol, The Tibetan Book of the Dead.*

I decided on my last birthday that I would celebrate my mom's life and my birth together. My children were with me. In Gestalt therapy, this kind of celebratory memorial is called "completion." I felt it was important for my children to see and hear what a loving, full life my mom had.

How do we do that exactly? How can we come to peacefully accept death as a natural, remarkable process? For me, a key step was the realization that a piece of our dearly departed stays with us.

I believe that when my mother died, some of her spirit, her energy, her life force — stayed with me. My friend Sally told me that she, too, felt a subtle energy enter through her solar plexus when her grandmother died. In the realm of the unseen, love is stronger than death. And I know that a big piece of my father lives inside of me and forms my character and my moral code to this very day.

Conversely the dying worry about leaving their loved ones behind. Many people are ready to leave but hang on because their families are not ready to let go. My father was concerned about departing so early. He didn't want to leave his wife and three children.

And their concerns are well-founded. I was only 19 years old, and, of course, I didn't want to let him go. His death meant that a cherished part of me was dying. Despite all the work I have done to understand and embrace death in a more spiritually mature and evolved way, I experienced that pain again when my mother died, more than 30 years later.

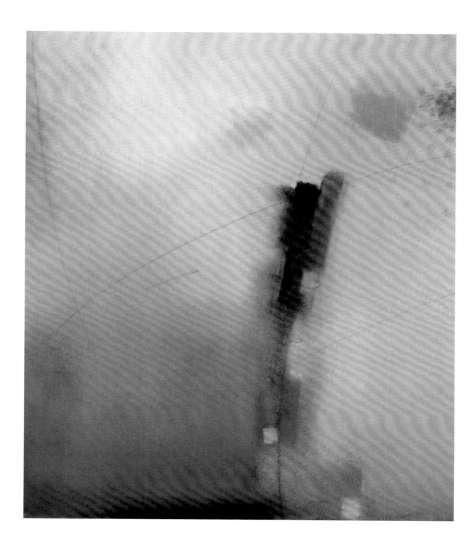

Over time, however, I have learned to "stay in touch" with them both regularly. In my personal meditations and spiritual practices, I move deeply into my heart and send love to my dad and mom. I let them know that my life is good, and that I remain grateful for their profound teachings. I find this process spiritually healing, and it serves as an opportunity for growth.

I also feel my meditations give comfort to those who have crossed over. Knowing I am well allows them to continue their soul work without worrying about me. My parents are now the subject of my truth. Their death taught me that our relationship can continue and their wise teachings continue for me. My heart tells me when they are speaking through others. I may sit next to someone on an airplane and receive pertinent information about a personal matter. I may think: "Mom, Dad, help me on this matter," and their wise thoughts and guidance show up for me — the person next to me will say something that will make me realize it's coming from my parents, speaking to me in a deep, profound way. If you pay attention to these signs, you will hear them.

By the same token, a mistake we make is that we believe we have forever and we postpone being with those we love the most. It is always later than we think. Every day, let's make a toast to those we love, wherever they may be!

And live fully in the moment. A life lived with faith, hope, charity and happiness is a quality life. The quality of the journey is what really matters.

Science and the Soul

Science and religion present two complex systems of thought regarding death. They both offer explanations, but each one is incomplete. Although science is ever evolving and expanding its scope, it still cannot definitively explain the soul, afterlife or even the beginning of life.

The most widely accepted theory of the origin of the universe is called the Big Bang Theory, which postulates that a "singularity" exploded (or, more precisely, "expanded") and brought the universe into being. The theory doesn't explain what it is exactly that "banged," where it came from or why it happened.

Science is still full of areas of interest that we have no understanding of whatsoever. Researchers often use the code word "dark" to talk about such phenomena. When you see the word "dark" in the field of science you may know that they are talking about something they can't understand — like dark matter or dark energy.

Is it possible that the dark matter in our universe — which has never been directly measured — could in part be made up of consciousness and the so-called spirit world?

Sir Isaac Newton, considered by many to be the greatest scientist who ever lived, described the mechanics of gravity and invented calculus in order to calculate the orbits of planets more accurately than anyone before him. He solved the mathematics of gravity, but didn't attempt to say what gravity actually was. That was left to Albert Einstein, whose brilliant theory of relativity completed the picture of the world.

Interestingly enough, it was Albert Einstein who proved that atoms really exist, and *that* is what he received the Nobel Prize for, not for E=MC^2 as most people assume.

It was left for the architects of quantum physics to examine the world of the atom and its subatomic particles. Quantum physics has shown us that we have a very long way to go indeed before we can say that we have a complete understanding of the physical nature of the universe.

Science is a continuous march from discovery to discovery, with each new discovery changing what we believe to be the truth about reality. I wonder if science may progress to a point where it can measure and quantify the afterlife? Will quantum mechanics be the answer, or at least part of it? Perhaps the quantum particles of consciousness will always stay connected and influence one another. If we have a soul, and it exists in the form of energy not yet known to physics, does that mean it does not exist? If you shared deep love and a soulful connection with another human being and that person dies, could it be that the love and soul connection also dies, or does it somehow stay alive — either in our hearts and minds or in a place, unknown to science, in our own cosmos?

The cells in our bodies are continually replaced. Do thoughts, feelings and memories, as non-cellular matter, outlast the body? Does love and consciousness then transcend our physical being?

Consider the Alternatives

Faith and tradition do offer moral guidance while we're here on earth, and they address the question of existence, as well as where our souls go when we die. Learning how science and religion can mesh in world traditions brings us toward additional answers about the afterlife. This is fundamental because we will always ask questions.

Science asks: "What is the origin of mankind; how did the world begin; how will it end?" When we carefully examine the two camps, science and religion — and there are examples of both in the quotes of this book — something fascinating begins to emerge. Science and religion, in all parts of the world, in aspects of work and avocation, seem to be pulling closer and closer.

His Holiness the Dalai Lama supports a cutting-edge exchange program at Emory University for scientists and contemplative monastics. I am certain that a major breakthrough in science and spirituality will arise from this meaningful exchange. The historically stiff line of differences will softly begin to blend. Perhaps the most interesting example of melding science and religion is the documentation of near-death experiences. Is death as divine as life, or is it better? What does "better" mean? Raymond Moody wrote a book called *Life After Life*. He interviewed hundreds of people who had near-death experiences and came back with new perspectives on life.

Tibetan Buddhists believe that after death, consciousness remains alive and we travel through various intermediate states, called *bardos*, in the interval between death and the next rebirth, *reincarnation*. Tibetans further believe that a dead person can still hear earthly voices for some time after death, and so it is their ritual to read the *Bardo Thodol* to the deceased to guide the dead person through the bardos to insure that they will be reincarnated as a human.

Reincarnation is a fundamental belief in Hinduism and Taoism, too. Plato endorsed versions of reincarnation. A friend who is an orthodox rabbi, once told me that he believes in reincarnation. Many leading Kabbalists feel the same way. In Christianity, Jesus' resurrection is, to me, a form of reincarnation. He rose again and appeared in the spirit form, first to Mary Magdalene and then to his disciples. Mary was the first to "see" him. *Perhaps Mary could access both realms simultaneously?*

Many other spiritual teachers believe the work of the soul continues on the other side. Even people who have hurt us, who were unkind or were parents we did not have a good relationship with can work with us to heal issues after they die. That's why it is so important that we find it within ourselves to forgive as well as be forgiven, even after death. If we harbor feelings of resentment toward one who has died, we should take the opportunity to heal and improve that relationship.

The late parapsychologist and researcher, Hans Holzer, once said: "Everything we have here — they have over there. That is a duplicate of this world, except over there the purpose is to develop the personality from the negative to the positive, or to give them assignments, or to send them down for some more education."

William James, the founder of modern psychology, maintained

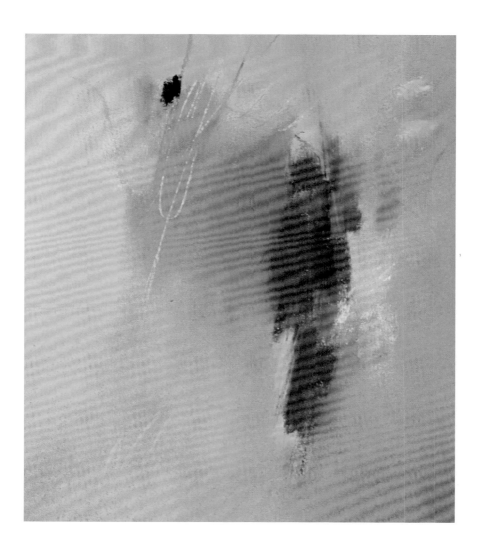

that our consciousness is fed by a cosmic immaterial realm into our brains. When our brains die, the consciousness carries on.

Lockhart McGuire, a professor of medicine in Virginia, took the concept a step further. McGuire was diagnosed with metastatic cancer. He was asked to address medical students about his condition and his impending death. "By whatever method the leap of faith occurs," he said, "it can be orienting during life and, in the face of death, possibly transcendent and even redemptive."

The pain and suffering that often go hand in hand with dying are understood by many as an enlightening part of the journey we make toward a developed concept of God, or however you wish to refer to a Supreme Being.

Alan C. Mermann, MD, a Christian, has served many people on their deathbeds. He believes we must recognize several fundamental segments of self-understanding in relationships with patients and their families as one is about to cross over. He writes:

"1. Does life have meaning? The shadow of death sweeps away easy answers and supports the alternative of considering anew the … human journey.

2. The major religions in Western culture stand firm in their faith in a life after death.

3. What will it mean to 'not be?' Our dying patients can raise those spiritual questions that have called to us for so many centuries... the roles of religious faith and the life of the spirit... provide meaning where chaos may seem to reign. Our hearts and minds can open to different realities….

4. ...our dying patients are ourselves farther along on a common journey.

5. As life comes to a close, persons require honesty from those who care for them, and open communication about what the future holds. Love, in its many forms, is a gift we can offer those who face death. The intimate relations between love and forgiveness suggest a role for the physician as advocate in resolution of conflicts.... An examined life may invoke a deep desire for forgiveness by God so that true peace may come at last."

At some point in our earthly existence, many individuals awaken to the concept that the most important part about life is that it is a stepping stone to death. The work of end-of-life experts Elisabeth Kubler-Ross and David Kessler, as well as Ondrea and Stephen Levine, has shown that we have so much to learn from the dying. As Kessler says, "The dying have always been teachers of great lessons, for it's when we are pushed to the edge of life that we see most clearly."

If you think of spirit, peace, love and death as four elements in a circle, you may envision a map of life. Death is equally as significant as the other three. Each year on November 2, Mexican tradition celebrates *el Dia del Muerto*, or the Day of the Dead. This is a time to remember family members who have died. Families bring food and flowers to honor their relatives. At night, they light candles and set up picnics near their departed ones' graves. The Day of the Dead isn't sad. It's a celebration, a way to reconnect to those who have entered a new dimension.

Perhaps death is moving into a silent realm of love and intimacy. As Robert Sardello states in his book *Silence*: "As we enter into Silence, we enter into Wisdom. We do not become wise but enter into the objective Wisdom of world processes. As we enter into the Wisdom of Silence, we allow ourselves to be taught by the things of the world. We allow the revelations that flow from the Silence to give rise to their thinking through us."

Silence helps us get in touch with our inner calm. It is a place where we can find emotional freedom, a place where we can deeply connect to our intuition. I believe we find many personal answers in silence and meditation.

As quoted by Thomas Merton and Johannes Tauler, adapted:

"O God, may I find deep solitude and gentleness with which I can truly love my brothers and sisters. For I know, O Lord, that the more solitary I am, the more affection I have for them. May solitude and silence teach me to love others for what they are, not for what they say. Give me your spirit to learn wisdom through humility, knowledge by letting go, how to speak by silence and how to live by dying."

What I Believe

We can't discount our own personal experience of truth. If you were to ask me, "How do you feel right now?" I am the only one who can answer that question accurately. There is no experiment that science can conduct or piece of equipment that can be used that will give a 100 percent reliable answer to that simple question. Yet inside me, I *know* beyond any doubt the exact answer

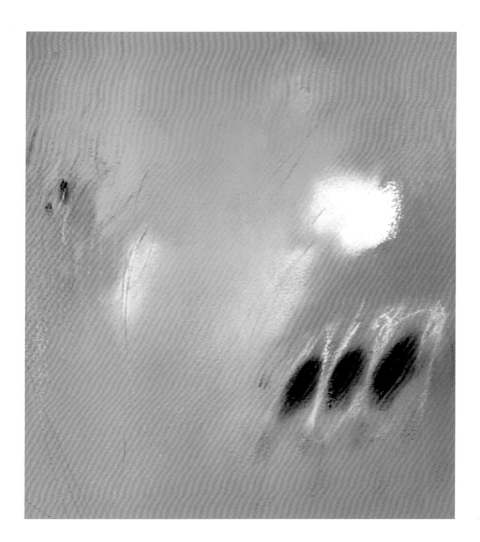

to that question and to countless others like it.

And this personal understanding is not limited to internal consciousness. The experience of seeing the rainbow in my office is just one example of things I see in nature that speak to me.

I have even felt that way about clouds. I love staring at clouds. I could look at them every day and never be bored. When I was a child, I would lie on the ground and look up at the clouds and imagine animal shapes, flowers and buildings. When the sunlight shines through them, they look like mystical kingdoms, islands or magical spheres. When I stare at clouds, my mind wanders. I think heavenly thoughts filled with dreams, wonder and awe.

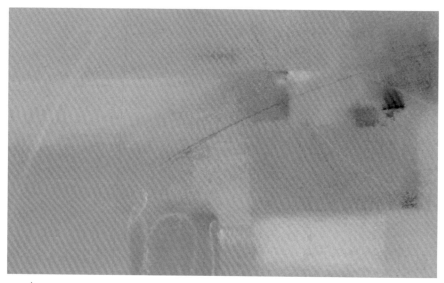

They stimulate my curiosity, my personal search for truth: Do they just float up in the sky and give the earth shade and rain, or do their shapes have meaning? Do clouds communicate a hidden message to us? Do they tell their own story or that of someone from beyond?

I have no definite answers, only beliefs that stem from personal faith and what I deem mystical evidence. In my personal search for truth, for God, the Divine, the Creator, it seems obvious that life is only one stage in the hierarchy of eternity. Life is a stepping stone to death. And after death we ask: Do we transcend the body, go to a timeless existence and find life everlasting?

The intransigent dualism of life and death is an earthly trapping. Our lives are made up of body, mind and soul. Body and soul are not dualistic, but they are different. Is it possible that they have distinct functions after death — one disintegrates while the other goes on? I deem our immaterial minds and hearts far removed, literally, from our material bodies; that the mortal fate of our physical body does not imply the death of our love, hearts and souls.

Like the Tibetans, I believe there is a time period in which there is a sacred, precious "hanging out" after physical death. There is change going on. I have felt the "presence" of close friends and family after their death. I had conversations in my heart and mind with them. I felt their souls were growing and changing before they agreed to their final departure from the Earth plane. For the pre-deceased, it is a time to be quiet. In contemplation, there can be felt a sense of the mystical meaning of the universe.

A Prescription for Death

As beings who possess a body, mind and soul, we tend to think of these three parts of ourselves as intertwined — until death. We see life and death as being an "either/or" concept — you are either dead or alive. But perhaps the body disintegrates yet the mind and soul go on and do not require a material home to survive?

I'm in that camp. I don't believe that the mortal end of the physical body brings death to the mind and soul. In fact, I believe the death of the body is a kind of freedom for the mind and soul to live on, and therefore, the love experienced by any soul survives infinitely. Although science and some religious traditions may refute it, to my mind, neither can absolutely "prove" it isn't that way. The evidence is, at best, incomplete.

Thus, the distinction between life and death is, at worst, relative. In deep meditation, it is possible to voluntarily visit the space that lives beyond time and live in the eternal now. That can be interpreted as dying before you die. Even as our childhoods die and we move through adolescence into adulthood, each stage of letting go will move us forward in wisdom so that we can love more fully and live our lives with empathy and compassion.

Another example of this relativity of the life cycle is when a loved one passes. A part of me died when my father and mother crossed over. Divorce, changing jobs or losing a pet bring pain to our hearts; they are mini-deaths. Yet, new lessons come forth and experiences unfold. We give birth to original thoughts and fresh ways of living as we work through pain and heartache, learning to adapt and expand.

Now and then you'll see denial in a family that is about to lose a loved one. Denial can temporarily shut down the love and heart connection, and one will miss the beauty of death. The greatest gift you can give someone who is dying is to impart loving permission to go. It takes courage and wisdom to know when to give permission to those we love to release and expand into the new realm. My mom used to say, "Life is for the living." When someone dies, we must live on and continue to love them.

I have written and performed several memorial services and they were each a celebration of life. People told touching stories about the deceased. We prayed, celebrated and looked at photographs that told a thousand words about the person who had died. In some cases, videos were shown as we laughed and reminisced. This type of dynamic remembrance is sacred and vital to the letting-go process. Loving memories keep our loved ones alive in our hearts.

Staying present opens up the vessels of remembrance, the great river of feeling and deep inner-knowledge. The Divine presence is always there and since we can connect with the infinite now, upon death we can let go and gently move into this Divine presence. Centering prayer and the welcoming practice have helped me to learn this letting-go, non-clinging process. Our ultimate letting go will be that sweet surrender back to Divinity itself.

The Universe is for us. When we take the first step, we are met with gratitude and trust. Something in us knows we are

Divine. There is no place where God stops and we begin. There is a natural flow of life. Nothing stands still.

Love and Death

Most of us will be asking two questions on our deathbeds: How much have I loved? How much have I been loved? It will not matter how much money we've made or how many things we've acquired. It may not even matter how often and to what degree we've experienced love in our lives, because love and death are interconnected; spiritual love lasts forever.

When I think about what I value most in life, I consider human beings, animals and my natural surroundings to be most precious. Things don't make me happy; love does. I love my family and friends, my cats and dogs and I love the tree that provides shade for me to sit beneath in the warm summer months. I love to give love, and receive it. Spiritual happiness is made by sharing our love. We can start with a child we love unconditionally, and then extend that love to family, friends and strangers.

Recognizing the preciousness of human life opens our hearts to connect deeply. None of us will live forever but the love we have extended and shared will continue — like a perfume that lingers in the air after we have left the room. My parents' love still lingers in my heart.

In my studies with the writer Cynthia Bourgeault, I have learned that our egos must diminish here on earth in order that we may know more about love. The moment our egos are pushed aside, our hearts will open and our world will be transformed. Through the surrender of ego, in making ourselves less important, dying will become a rebirth. We are flowing out of the eternal state of things and upon death I suspect we will flow back to this eternal state.

As we drop deeper into our divine self, by letting go and finding who we really are, we discover our sacred strengths. The most important gift we can give one another is the pure transparency of our present. Our beauty lives in the quality of our aliveness.

If we can live out of the place where there is no time, we connect to infinity. Our beautiful human self is the vessel in which the infinite manifests. When it is our time to cross over, we can go courageously or kicking and screaming — it's our choice. We can choose to live — and die — consciously.

Our heart is the ultimate space traveler. The electromagnetic field of love and relatedness connects us to all, back to the source, and we do not fall out of it when we die. We are all beloved creatures flowing from Divinity and someday we will gently flow back to Divinity. Love never dies.

Ask yourself, "What is Death?" Your answer might just teach you how to live.

Lexie Brockway Potamkin

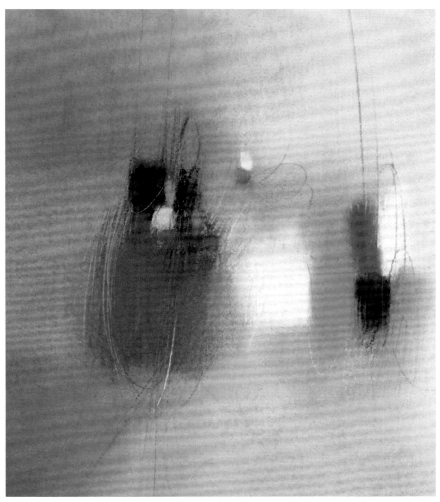

xliii

WHAT IS DEATH?

Responses from People of All Backgrounds

"Death is just another turn of the wheel in the endless and eternal cycle of birth and death.

We come in, we go out; where we come from and where we go are mysteries on the earth plane. Our essence is spiritual and I believe that when our bodies physically die, our souls, which are the true essences of ourselves, return to the place from which they originate. Our spiritual life force, by which we are all connected to our Creator, lives on in perpetuity."

Adrienne Levin, Trademark law administrator

"I learned at an early age that death is a formidable adversary.

Death stole my sister away after she gave birth to her baby son when she was only 24, and I was turning 15.

I expected that death would take my grandparents when they grew old. Even now — fighting back my tears as an adult orphan — I knew the time would come one sad day when death would claim my mother and father. Death has shortened the lifetimes of so many others I've loved — friends, lovers and family members with the story lines of airplane and automobile crashes, suicides, cancer, medical malpractice and more.

In the 1934 film 'Death Takes a Holiday' starring Frederic March and Evelyn Venable, and in the 1971 remake starring Yvette Mimieux and Monte Markham, Death decides to walk the earth for a few days disguised as a mortal human being, here to learn why people fear him — while they continue to take everyday life for granted. Little does Death know that he'll find love and discover why mortals fear the thought of endings and the finality of loss of life. A 'broken heart' and 'gone forever' are new 'mortal' concepts that Death takes with him as he departs, becoming a dark force again, changing and taking lives.

I am of two minds when it comes to dealing with death.

As a middle-aged mother, I would like to cheat death for as long as possible. It's my divine wish to stay healthy and age gracefully — watching my precious teenage daughter grow up and have a happy and joyous life, and that I may continue to be an important part of it for decades to come.

But as gently as I go, if it were at all possible or necessary to hunt down Death before it got to me, I, like everyone else would be happy to be packing a .357 Magnum."

Arlene W. Leib, PR, media relations

"Death is not something to fear. When we die, we leave this physical body, with all the pain, the sickness and the heartaches that afflict us all. We are given new bodies in Heaven that have none of the afflictions we have on earth.

I know my mother came to me after she died. She was no longer suffering from cancer. She looked and felt wonderful, reunited with her mother who died shortly after childbirth. The place she showed me, which I cannot find the words to describe, which I know was Heaven, is like nothing we can even begin to imagine.

I know when it is my time to die, I will go where I can sit at my Master's feet and just bask in His eternal love. Yes, someone comes to meet you when you die, whether a family member or one of God's Angels.

I have been with loved ones as they passed from this earth, only to hear them tell of someone here with them, waiting for them to go with that person or Angel. The look of pure joy on those faces was beyond any joy I have seen on anyone else.

As the song goes, I can only imagine."

Anna Breedlove, Disabled

3

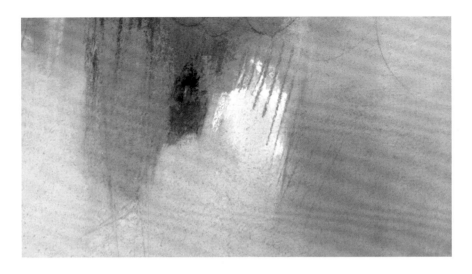

"As an oncologist, I am often asked how I personally deal with 'losing' a patient. To my knowledge I have never lost one, as I know exactly where they are.

Of course all survivors after a death of a loved one will experience a huge sense of loss. But being a doctor I find myself an unwilling participant in a vast army of health care providers in a crusade against death. We battle cancer, heart disease and an endless myriad of illnesses and injuries. Often we are successful in these skirmishes but the outcome of the 'war' is ultimately inevitable.

If you live, you must also die. Certainly I believe that medical practice should be directed first to prevention and then, in face of an illness, provide the best treatment available in order to reach the highest quality of life obtainable. That means educating the patient and family to the nature of their illness with a realistic treatment upside, risk and downside. Sometimes that means limiting treatments to symptoms and supportive care.

The true problem is death isn't our enemy. Failing to live life to the fullest is. I recently consulted with a young woman who was discovered during her pregnancy to have a very advanced incurable breast cancer. Treatments were appropriately withheld until the birth of her young son. She received the most powerful chemotherapy and radiation treatments available for four months, but despite this her cancer continued to progress. She knows she has fought hard trying to regain her health. She thinks that she may die soon, although she is confused by her physician's insistence that she can make it. Her cancer has created lymph edema, severe swelling, of her arm and hand. This has made it very difficult for her to care for and carry her baby.

After listening to her, we discussed videotaping her hopes and dreams for her young son. We discussed creating additional family time with 'mini-vacations' from treatments. I also suggested lymph edema therapy which is a gentle pressure massage and a special sleeve to reduce the swelling so she may hold her child. Her medical oncologist actually told her, 'No!' His fear is that the sleeve and massage may further induce spreading. He also feels she must stick with the strict protocols for her best chance. He doesn't want to lose his fight against death and is willing to do whatever it takes. He, I believe fails at what should be his primary goal: to help her and her family live life to the maximum for whatever time she may have left.

Although I'm not opposed to her trying additional therapies, realistically, she is going to die soon. But because her physician is holding on, she is, too, except not to her child. She would like to create some joy in her life away from the endless labs, X-rays and doctors. This story of fighting death — no matter what — isn't unique. It's ubiquitous. There needs to come a time when the objective of defeating death needs to be redirected to compassionate care focusing on the quality of remaining life and the issues involving dignity.

I'm frequently asked if I believe in rebirth or an afterlife. The origin and nature of consciousness, despite years of scientific exploration, remains unclear and speculative, without any proof if consciousness continues to exist, or not, after death. Whether a person, a species or a star, death can occur only if something exists. Nothingness, on the other hand has never existed. Therefore, it stands to reason, something exists, even after death. Your guess is as good as mine. But I do know that because of death, life is the most precious and miraculous of all gifts. Those very special lives that have embraced me and are no longer physically present — like my brother and my parents — will live within me for the remainder of my life and bring me an eternal song of joy."

Alan Tralins, Radiation oncologist,
director, Bardmoor Cancer Center

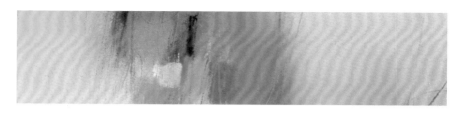

"Is death a beautiful end or a fresh, new start?

Is it dark to be scared from, or it is light where all the good souls go?

It's all those things that we grow up with...nothing to be afraid off or to be scared from. It's what it is. Life after death, or death after life? Each death is different, each person leaves a different life, each soul has a different ending.

Death comes with life. Just look around and open your heart and eyes."

Andrea-Noemi Bredak, Artist

"What is death? The answer depends upon the person. For some it is a blissful altered state. For others it is meeting a departed loved one. For some it is a sense of the beauty of nature.

And sometimes near the end, people say, like the physicist Richard Feynman, it is 'not something you want to go through twice.'"

Arnold Mindell, Author, *Coma, Key to Awakening*

"Death is separation from all that is earthly and known to man on this side.

Death is moving into eternity and spending it one of two places, heaven or hell. Death brings awareness of all things, and in death the mystery of God, good and evil is solved, once and for all."

Atonya Clark, Entrepreneur

"I received the request to comment about death, coincidentally, on the 22nd anniversary of my mother's crossing into spirit. It's a day when I take extra time to communicate with her. I am completely confident that she hears me.

Shortly after she crossed over, my mother began to visit me. Much to my surprise, because she died prematurely and suddenly, I discovered that she, too, had to adjust being on the other side. Clearly, she was expecting to come home from the hospital to her earthly life, not her spiritual life.

I frequently had dreams of my mother and my grandmother being together right after her crossing. These were not ordinary dreams; they were visits. For me they were very real.

One time, about a month or two after she passed away, I was teaching a channeling class at a client's home in Virginia. I was asleep in the guest room when my mother's spirit appeared. She lay down in the bed next to me and put her arms around me. We both lay there, embracing each other, weeping deeply. I don't know how long this lasted, but it was profound. It never occurred to me that she too, might also be sad at the loss. It has been many years since her crossing, and the sadness of the loss has been replaced by the solace of her presence in my life.

My mother visits me from time to time, especially when I am going through a difficult passage in life. She never says anything, but her presence is always comforting. Death is a gateway into the spirit world, the place that is our true home. As a medium who is constantly moving in and out of my physical form, I am aware of the beauty of the 'other side.' My spirit guides teach that death is no more than a transition from the physical plane to that of the infinite, or the spirit world.

The concept of death is a frightening one for most people because they do not understand their own essence as a spirit being. We move in and out of incarnation, or the embodiment of a physical form, for a limited period of time. Because we are, in essence, spirit, it is organic for us to come and go from the spirit realm to the temporary lodging of the physical. If we reverse our concept to understanding our true nature as spirit, then the inevitability of death is not one that we must face with trepidation. At the same time, the eventual demise of our physical form assists us in appreciating our life. We see our physical life as the opportunity to learn, grow and evolve. It is said that death is always looking over our shoulder. The time we spend in form is precious. We must appreciate life for its singular purpose, to awaken to who we truly are as spirit beings."

Asandra, Artist, author

"Death is the beginning of our spiritual journey just as birth is the beginning of our physical journey.

As end of life approaches, we see so many working to reach a conclusion to their physical time on earth. We see the gathering of friends and family. We witness the completion of tasks to ensure the well-being of those left behind, finishing whatever is left undone. We see the mending of fences, the joyful reunions.

The end of life is a time we make peace with ourselves, our loved ones and whatever or whoever we believe in. It is a time of saying goodbye to what we know and love and accept the new journey we are about to embark on.

I have not experienced death, but I know from looking into the eyes of those passing on that death is not to be feared. I know from being present at multiple hospice patients' bedsides that there is something beyond this life we know. I know that at the time of death, the physical body ceases all function. The spirit, however, lives on. I know this as surely as I know my name. I heard my grandmother after she passed, I have felt the hug of patients when their bodies were too weak to move.

Death is a new beginning."

Barbara Kircher, Administrator, Hospice Advantage

"Death is a transformation from one way of being into another. In a horoscope, I would be very hard pressed to find a 'death pattern,' because such a pattern would look very much like other key transformational patterns one finds in a birth chart. This is because our essential being — our essence, if you will — continues to live on in other realms long after the physical body has died.

Sometimes it is possible for someone who has died to communicate with someone still in the body. And often we are able to 'see' our death — the tunnel with the light at the end we're so familiar with in near-death experiences. It's very important to remind ourselves that we are first and foremost souls having a physical experience, rather than the other way around.

Death is not a fearsome thing, although we humans are geared to fear change. It's the end of one way of being and a new beginning. It's part of our soul's great learning journey."

Barbara Dini, Caretaker

"As a pagan, I see death as a different state of being.

It's a very mysterious state of being where we are perhaps conscious, but in another way. I'm forever curious about how people who die 'wake up' and see where they have landed and what their new world is.

How do people who die suddenly and with no preparation-- as in murder or fatal accidents — feel when they find themselves on 'the other side?' Unless we believe in mediums, of course, it's hard to know until we get there ourselves. I don't personally know anyone who's been there and come back or even sent verifiable messages back to us.

Who is in this other place? Family and friends waiting to greet us? Our gods and goddesses? I also see reincarnation as a concept that makes enormous sense; so perhaps death is like summer vacation between grades in school. We rest and recreate (in two senses of that word) and then come back for our next life.

I had a near-death experience in 1992 after a severe asthma attack. Two friends took me to the ER. I remember seeing the glass doors, and then I was floating around just under the ceiling of the ER watching the clock on the wall move v-e-r-y slowly, and then a doctor or nurse was calling my name and I opened my physical eyes. I was told I'd been 'gone' for 20 to 30 minutes, but all I remember clearly is that clock. I didn't go down a tunnel, I didn't see light, I didn't hear voices. I came back with my faculties fully intact."

Barbara Ardinger, PhD, Author, book editor

"Death is the single point at which one form of life ends and one begins in another realm.

As we age, our physical form declines as our spiritual form becomes increasingly enriched and fulfilled. At the point of death, we are transformed from flesh and bones to oneness in spirit as we move through to the journey at the next level.

I don't believe that our spirit completely leaves this realm, but that it is able to navigate several. We live on in the spirit into eternity. In that respect, I guess we die into life."

Barbara Owen, Broker associate

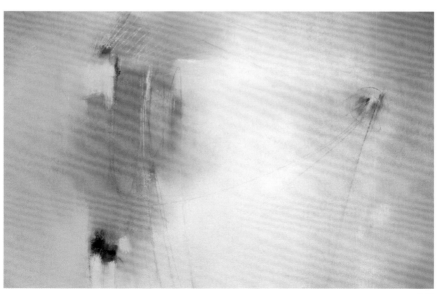

"I don't know what is death. I only know what I believe it isn't.

I believe death is something other than what I see, sense and experience every day of my life. I don't know if death is something better, something less or a variation of the life I live today. I just don't believe it is exactly what I have or who I am today.

This understanding came to me the day I was diagnosed with breast cancer. I fully realized for the first time that my life could be shorter than I planned. Death presented itself to me, getting right in my face, as you might say. I already knew that I loved life, but now life garnered from me the special respect it deserves.

My daughter was only four. I loved being her mom. I lived a good life, worked for nonprofit projects I felt were valuable, was in a place that I loved and had a richness of friends beyond measure. Every day inspired me with something wondrous. I didn't want to leave any of this. This is not to say that my life was without its challenges. But facing the possibility of not having life opened my eyes wide to it.

This is the gift of cancer.

Then the thought came to me one day as I was driving for my daughter's pre-school carpool. I had finished eight rounds of chemo and would soon begin radiation. I had lost all my hair. On this particular day as I drove the girls home, they became very cranky and very loud. And I had to stop at the grocery store, taking three crying kids in with me and was wearing an ill-fitting wig. I thought to myself, is this what I am working so hard to stay alive for? The answer came to me immediately — yes, absolutely! I knew with great gratitude that yes, this is it. Every bit of it. Thankfully, I have life beyond cancer, and the gifts it brought me.

My daughter is now ten. There are still plenty of times when I roll my eyes at the difficulties of the day and with a smile and think, yes, this is it."

Carlyle Kyzer, Nonprofit development

"I was with my father when he passed, and with pets, and what I witnessed was the cessation of individual life as we know it: breath and bodily systems stopped and the personalities ceased to be in those forms. But who's to say death is the end? Certainly the 'dead' live on in our hearts and minds, which is where we met them in the first place when we experienced them as being among the living. So we are not simply bodies. We live through others as thought.

I am as you experience me to be, a story. 'I' is a story. 'You' is another story. 'She' and 'he' are fairy tales concocted by minds. 'They' are yet another yarn spun out of the mind. Life and death are also stories.

Bodies apparently die; can that which animates them ever die? I don't know the answer, but my suspicion — and I hope I'm correct — is that it's one life, expressed through many."

Carol Skolnick, Author, facilitator

"The outbreath empties. Nothing left.
Time stops. The stillness deafens. Void
is endless, dark and swirled. The force
of energy and matter presses on.
Deep breath is shared, not mine.
Your life continues, mine in yours.
We only know the present here.
We're one. No words — experience."

Bo Persiko, Professor, psychologist

"Being a spiritual healer for the past 20 years has given me the opportunity to face life and death personally and professionally.

As a hospice volunteer for a year, I learned how to live my life more authentically — to live each day more fully before taking that final breath. My mother was 95 years old when she took her final breath. I was by her side, chanting some ancient Hawaiian chants for an hour after she passed. I could see a vapor-like substance leave her body and linger for a moment on the shelf above her head.

The entire day had been dark and stormy. But at that moment, the sky opened up with sunshine showering light upon my mother's face. Her body was gone, but I'm sure that the essence that was my mother was taken into that light.

I saw it!

It validated my belief that our bodies only 'house' our soul for

16

a lifetime or the length of a dream. Earth is our kindergarten to learn how to love more fully while we're in the body. When we're finished we get to return to our real home — the Light.

I was blessed with having my mother for 60 years of my life before she passed. Losing my only son at 30 years old was truly heartbreaking. Our children are supposed to outlive us. Death, this time, filled me with grief at the loss of my child. Yet after many months, the grief lifted and filled me with peace that his soul was truly in a happier place.

I see people 'dying a thousand deaths' every day because of fear-based beliefs. My mission in life is to raise the consciousness of how to forgive ourselves from the past and live totally in the present."

Belinda Farrell, Hypnotherapist, spiritual healer

"It's the point when an interrelated system of processes such as blood circulation, breathing, digestion, brain function and so on that are not normally associated with disease processes have all come to an end."

Bill Bell, Career development practitioner

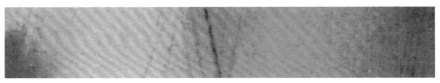

"Death is the transition into heaven where we will see our departed loved ones and experience the peace and love that we so wanted in our earthly life.

We will be surrounded by the ultimate love and light of God."

Beverly Love, Senior admissions advisor

"Death is the loss of one's soul's earthly container. It is a release into a higher realm where you become a part of the larger plan, free of earthly burdens."

Carolie Collins, Social worker, adult crisis team

"Death is the natural end to life. It is a crossing over for the soul or spirit or life energy. There is a hereafter. Heaven or hell; I cannot say.

I do believe that there is reincarnation, since as a young baby I experienced a visit to my former family in a dream or astral projection. I don't tell that to very many people since I don't want to be perceived as crazy."

Christine, Student

"Death is life and life is death.

Now that I have come full circle I can, yes, live! For me, and from the lessons of a living that continues at this time, I see death and life as two sides of the same coin. Therefore, I am not weighted down with a debilitating fear of the unknown and am free to expand and explore the fullness of each moment, moment by moment, of my life.

I choose to see death through the eyes of my heart, which is a remarkable point from which to view all that living entails. Somehow, and of course I cannot be sure even when feeling completely at home with the idea, I sense the eternity of joy as forever present within my moment-to-moment choices. From here I can see all that matters."

Constance McClain, Educator

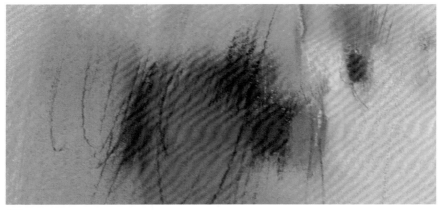

"Our life force that keeps us alive leaves the body, usually because the body can no longer function. This energy is spread out by the wind. It affects plants, animals and all the elements, just as sunlight and fire do.

Our energy can travel infinite distances, depending on the movement in the universe that takes it there. I have no idea what happens to consciousness. We'll have to wait to find that out.

Our body decays, and the people close to us whom we leave behind go through a grief process. They make decisions about what happens to us and often have a death ritual to celebrate our life or mourn. Hopefully people will eventually use nontoxic ways to return our bodies to the earth so that we can nourish future life with the nutrients in us."

Claire Noelle Frost, Green organizing coach

"Sweet sleep, sweet slumber, sweet death — a peace I've been waiting for all my life — sweet forgetfulness and dreams of only blissful quiet at last. No distracting sounds inside my head or out. No feelings of pain, of terror, of hate; no rushes of fear, of lust, of confrontation.

Take me away, my lord. Take me home from whence I came. I don't know the source — only that it is supremely beautiful.

It doesn't end here. It goes on and on in infinite spirit."

Clara Klein, Writer

"Death is the physical dissolution of the physical body, the ultimate defeat of order by entropy. This means the end of physical functioning as well as normal mental functioning.

I also believe that the physical body, as all of the material universe, is consciousness. The universe is a creative force that in some senses cannot be reduced to the basic laws of chemistry and physics. All is divine, and that divinity exists in each of us.

Where does that divinity go when we physically die? What is that divinity? These are big questions, and to say that we merge back into the universal consciousness — which I believe may approximate Truth — only approaches them.

How does this persistence move on? Many religious systems assume some form of reincarnation. However, I'm not sure that our personal memories and personalities are very important in the merging. I do not have any personal experiences suggesting past lives for myself. I also believe that knowing the finality of death is an important motivation for taking the lives we now hold seriously, to seize each day as an opportunity to further our understanding and help of others in this life.

Death is a part of that creative process."

Dr. David Lee, Botanist

"Death, to me, is somewhat of a mystery. It always amazes me that people spend more time planning for a vacation to the shore than planning for their death.

The older I get and the more I read and experience, the more I feel it is just a transition no different than birth. A baby goes from one state of being through a traumatic and possibly painful experience to exist in an entirely different state.

I believe our death and possible rebirth will be greatly influenced by our mental and spiritual attitude. If we have a positive, peaceful and compassionate attitude with few regrets, our death can be a meaningful and amazing experience.

If we are angry, agitated, regretful and afraid, it will be a very painful, horrid experience — again, much like childbirth. If you learn about childbirth, practice and prepare for it and feel confident before going into it, it will still be unfamiliar territory and you can only prepare so much for something like it.

Sometimes I wonder, when I read about near-death experiences, if maybe the tunnel and the light and the people calling to the person who is dying isn't just childbirth — down the birth canal, into the brightly lit room and into the waiting arms of attendants and parents.

I don't know. But in the meantime, I am working on learning how to make myself calm, peaceful and joyful so that when the time comes it will be as good as it can possibly be — and maybe the crowning moment of my life."

Debra Burleigh, Technical writer, editor

"Several years ago we created a video installation for an exhibition called 'The Missing Peace: Artists Consider the Dalai Lama.' The exhibition had called on artists to pick one of a number of Buddhist themes, and we chose impermanence.

The reasons for our choice were many, but we were probably most affected by an experience we had while filming for a project about a cancer survivor. She was a bright, vibrant woman who had confronted her disease with great courage and humanity. When we started, she had seemingly won her fight and was eager to share her experience with others.

We spent a month interviewing her, her friends and her husband about what they had learned from her struggle. Then, about halfway through our work, her cancer virulently returned and took her from us. This experience led us to wonder if others had similar stories about impermanence in its most extreme form: death. We set out with a vague plan. We'd turn on our cameras and ask people to talk about the topic. It took only one interview to learn that we had struck a chord. While few people talk openly with one another about impermanence, we learned that many had thought deeply about the subject. In subsequent interviews, we were surprised by how wise people could be when they finally decided to address this subject.

It wasn't merely the religious and spiritual thinkers who proved the most interesting. One of our best interviews was with a man who had come by our house to wash our windows. He was from Jamaica and because we had a little difficulty with each other's accents, he didn't immediately understand what we meant by 'impermanence.' While we were explaining it, he suddenly said, 'Oh, you mean, you are on fire.' We thought, what a great way to talk about impermanence.

In the end, it was responses like his that helped make our installation what it was. We presented all of the interviews, edited by topic, in a circle of video iPods. Sometimes their voices spoke collectively; at other times, a single voice could be heard above the rest. The effect allowed viewers to listen in, just as we had, to 122 people talking about impermanence.

We published a book and DVD of the project titled *Impermanence, Embracing Change*. It presented the ideas of those we interviewed, together with topical essays by a number of prominent thinkers. We were not trying to draw any conclusions. Instead, the words and images hopefully allow one to listen and perhaps take part in a discussion about impermanence.

Like our subjects, you may find that while you rarely speak openly about this topic, you have thought about it very much indeed."

David Hodge, Artist, filmmaker, designer

"Death is the end of a physical reality but not of our eternal consciousness."

Fernando J. Valverde, MD, Physician

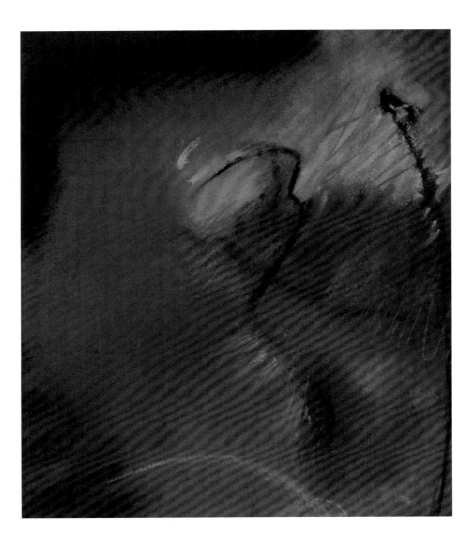

"I believe that all through life we experience 'small deaths,' and I now see them as preparation of sorts for the death of the body in this realm.

We experience these small deaths as change, such as anything or event that makes us move from what we have thought, known or accomplished. Through change, we are forced to leave something behind that we won't see or experience again. For example, divorce from a loved partner. The partner is still alive, but your life together and that person is dead to you except in memory. One must go forward.

We experience death as leaving a time of life — from childhood to adulthood — from adulthood to our last stage in life. That's when we have to leave behind what we have experienced or known to go forward into the unknown challenges of the next stage.

When we leave this realm we are going back to the space from whence we came. As a believer of an afterlife, death of the body is seen as a release from the challenges of this realm. In the Christian scriptures we are promised an everlasting life."

Shirley Henly, Executive director,
English Speaking Union, Houston branch

"Death is Neiman Marcus, but with Walmart prices."

Steve Young, Comedian

"I experienced death. I died briefly during surgery a few years ago. I had just lost my sixth baby during premature labor.

The first reaction I had was one of complete freedom. I felt weightless. And I was happy. Mentally I heard a male voice; I saw no one. I was instructed to 'think' flying. Wow, instantly I was floating. What a free feeling, what a wonderful way to move. Mentally, again, I was told to follow. I soon found myself floating over the back door of my home. I witnessed my husband telling my children that mommy didn't make it this time. I was crushed to see their faces. Before I could say anything I was told to follow again. This time I found myself on the very top of a black, crusty mountain. I looked in every direction, nothing. A big void. I looked up, nothing. A quiet that was deafening. I was asked if I wanted to stay. I began remembering the heartache of my baby dying. I remembered I didn't have anyone that really loved me.

Then, mentally, I was told that death was my choice; however, I would have to remain in this big, black void for eternity. Well, I could do it. I had enough of this life, this pain. I was finished. I was preparing myself to stay. Then a voice said, one of your children will feel responsible for your death and will not recover.

At that moment I decided I wanted to live again — not for me, but for my child. The following morning my doctor sat beside me in bed and asked me to tell her everything that happened during surgery.

How did she know? Before I could relate my story, she told me I was her first death. She described feeling my life force drain in her fingertips. She told me of feeling a dark, strong power pull me away from her.

She said she pulled me upright and shouted that she would be damned if I chose to die. Then she said, 'Tell me where you went.' I have watched dear seniors die in a nursing home, joyous and happy, with 'friends' coming to get them.

I discovered a very powerful force knows my deepest love, and only a small mention of me being blamed for a painful life was exactly what gave me the will to live another day."

Deborah Friend, Caregiver

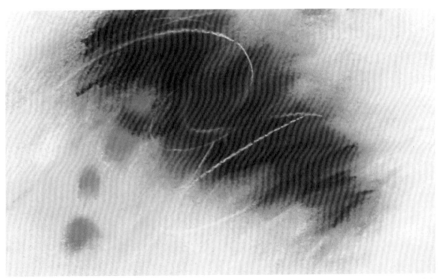

"The end of our physical life is much like the beginning of our existence. We have no knowledge of where we came from and certainly cannot determine a place in which we are to go.

We try too hard to make reason of this because of our desires; we must have a purpose to fulfill. We create the life we live on earth. We determine if it is heaven or hell by the choices we make and how we chose to live our lives. We dream up salvation. We say that no matter what we do, or how we do it, there is redemption if you believe in this religion.

You may go somewhere wonderful when you die and be surrounded by all those you've loved. Perhaps God will be waiting for you to welcome you in with loving arms. But all too often the expectations of organized religion are too far out of reach and even harder to understand, with contradictions that many spend lifetimes trying to explain.

With all the amazing wonders we have all around us — the beauty of nature, the unexplainable universe, the sheer will of humankind. We need not complicate our thoughts but rather think more simply about what happens to us when we die. We are all great energy before birth, during life and after in death. How we nurture our energy in this life dictates how our energy is put back in to the cycle.

Reincarnation is possible through energy. One person can have intimate insight into another person's past life if their energy somehow generates through the other person. We never leave; we are always here — even if we present ourselves in different forms."

Crystal Judge, Nanny

"It has been a very long time since someone I was close to had died. However, this past weekend I lost my grandmother.

My family and I were there with her until the very end. I knew for her it was for the best, but for my dad, oh how it hurt. I had never known my dad to cry and it hurt me to see him in such agony. I did not know how to ease his pain. He had lost his father so long ago and now it was his mother's time.

As we all sat there wondering what was keeping grandma on this earth, my dad stated, 'I have yet to tell her goodbye.' At that moment my sister and I knew the answer. My grandma was waiting for my dad to say goodbye and to release her from this world into the next.

Now we knew what we had to do. We spoke with our dad and told him had to do this for grandma; she needs to be at peace and know that you will be fine.

After many hours he did just that and then soon afterwards she was gone.

You ask what is death? I think it is different for everyone. We all hold our own thoughts and beliefs; however, for me it is simply going home."

Debra Jones, Clinical service manager

"Death is simply returning from where we were before birth."

Trish Fraser, Retired

"Our precious Daddy had a massive heart attack at his chiropractor's office. He'd had one 20 months before in our den. He died and they brought him back. We saw him go through so much, but he was a fighter, a Marine. For thirteen days, we had him on life support.

I had asked him what happened when he died. He said he was right there and that he could hear everything. He said he saw a bright, beautiful, Christmas tree. It had these angel decorations on it and they kept getting brighter. Then all of a sudden the tree disappeared, and the angels were all around his bed. He looked at the clock on the wall, and there was the Virgin Mary smiling at him. He also saw my little brother Mitch, who had died twenty-six years earlier, smiling at him. He told my mother he saw Jesus.

I know the minute his heart quit beating, it began to beat in mine. I am not scared to die anymore, because I know when the times comes that God, Jesus, the holy spirit, Virgin Mary, the angels and my Daddy and little brother will be standing there with their arms open wide to take my hand and lead me home."

Debra Olguin Murphree, Stylist

"Your spirit is full of light reflecting beauty from inside of you out to the world. May you live a life of love with peace filling your soul.

Death is the doorway to the next dimension. Through grace, God holds out his hand to lead you to the other side."

Dee Jensen, Integrative health care

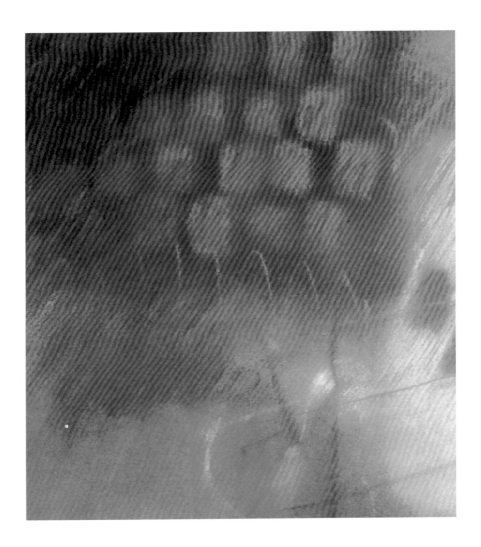

"The passing from one conscious experience to the next.

The return of spirit to its original phase of being which now has gained new insight, knowledge and awareness from the life experience of its latest earthly existence. Learning from the time here to have more compassion and understanding. To be able to experience love in it purest form.

If there is time, death teaches what is truly important, to 'see' loved ones and accept them as they are and to know what is really important. The good one has done for others, giving of one's self to help and realize is what matters.

When one passes, the opportunity of gaining understanding, to learn the answer to why things were the way they happened.

To become wise and gain peace. The gift of helping those who are left behind in ways one could not while here on earth, through inspiration, guidance and spiritual support, while respecting God's gift of free will for those here on earth to choose how to live their lives."

Dee Colon, Coordinator, managed health care

"Life has an expiration date. I recently learned that.

As young people we don't of think what our eventual fate will be. I know that we begin dying from the day that we are born.

I believe that death is the passage from this life into another. As we take our last breath, and our hearts take that last beat I think that our souls are pulled from the burden of the heavy body and released to float for a short time.

I have been at funerals and felt the presence of the dead one, and have been at other funerals and felt that dead one has already moved on.

Maybe we are given the choice to remain for a while, or leave when we are ready. I also think that we can come back after we are gone but I am not sure for how long.

I smelled my daughter's perfume one night as she passed through my bedroom. And I have days that I seem to find a lot of pennies. I read that is a common greeting from a loved one. I also believe that my loved ones are without pain, or fear, or anxiety or any of the common stuff we deal with here in our current state.

I think that heaven is what we want it to be, maybe fields of wheat, or rows of sunflowers or oceans with waves. But whatever it is, it is peaceful and full of love.

I lost my mother on October 25, 2009, and my daughter two days after I buried my mother. I know that they wait for me. I pull my strength from my mother and from God to get me through this pain that I feel here on earth. I know where I will go when my turn comes and I have no fear of death.

To me it is not death, just a new beginning, with those who have gone on first."

Denise Jones, Nurse

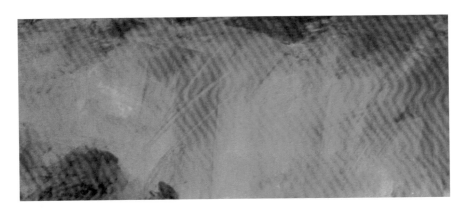

"Death is the continuation of the essence of what makes us.

The moment of death is a transition to a form of energy. Each person's experience may differ, based on belief. Death isn't a punishment or an end. It isn't a long rest. It's truly a new adventure that can continue without an end.

Death is, in many ways, like life. When a child is born, we celebrate a new life but spirits are saddened to lose them on the other side. When someone here dies we mourn the loss, but the spirits celebrate their arrival.

Death is a window to endless possibilities and wonderful journeys. When we die we do not encounter pain, judgment or damnation. We see what we wish to see, we do what we wish to do. There are endless possibilities on what the afterlife holds for us, and death is just the beginning."

Dominick Villella, Paranormal investigator

"My father had a massive coronary, was dead three minutes and came back to life. This is how he explained it:

'I was out of my body looking down on the doctors and nurses applying electric paddles to my chest to start my heart pumping again. I was surrounded by white light and felt very peaceful and serene. I also heard an 'angel' urging me to come to the 'other side' (heaven). I knew it was my choice as to whether I wanted to leave this earth or stay with my beloved family. It took a few minutes to make this decision since I was enjoying an experience that I had never had before. However, when I saw my wife and children grieving, I immediately chose life.'

I would like to add that my father lived happily and without fear for another 17 years.

Death, in my belief, is a joyous occasion; the end of our journey in this reality passing over to another dimension. Even though the physical body dies, relationships are eternal. They never die. It is my experience that, by being aware, I can access the souls of departed loved ones for solace, advice and guidance. There is no separation of our souls. The deceased goes to a home without suffering, anger, and loneliness. A home where only love and joy abound."

Donna L. Wiedinmyer, Entrepreneur, investor, mother

"Life is about loss."

Beverly Hayden, Rabbi

"Death is a beginning.

What a comfort to not just wish…. or hope…. but to know that life goes on after physical death.

In my nearly 40 years as a practicing parapsychologist, I have witnessed and experienced many paranormal life-after-life occurrences that have confirmed the existence of the soul after the event we call death.

The loving connection that we have with loved ones in this life continues to nourish, protect and replenish those who are still on this plane after their transition or passing.

Opening our hearts and minds to the many realities that exist around us gives one a sense of optimism, joy and lack of fear of the unknown. So, death is a beginning. Another path to go down in this individual journey we call life."

Dorothy Thau, Parapsychologist, healer, holistic health counselor, teacher, lecturer

"…the total emptiness for ever,
The sure extinction that we travel to
And shall be lost in always. Not to be here,
Not to be anywhere,
And soon; nothing more terrible, nothing more true."

From *Aubade* by Philip Larkin

Jay Gold, Senior vice president, chief medical officer

"I view death as part of the life spectrum and a transition from one plane of existence to another.

My work as a social worker, interfaith minister and bereavement counselor/educator has given me the gift of being present at the time of the passing of clients and loved ones. I was there with my husband and father when they each died.

As I am writing this, I am sitting at the bedside of my mother in a hospice program in Florida. It's a patchwork quilt of emotions, as I have moved from tears of anticipatory loss, imagining my life without her, to gratitude that I get to spend time with her, regardless of the duration. I do believe that the soul that we are, goes on in some form.

I have experienced after-death communication from loved ones who have passed, so I know that this life is not all there is. I have no fear of my own death and rather than feeling that the subject is morbid, I see it as an opportunity to appreciate everyone in my life.

Before my husband died in the '90s, I was engaged in what I called 'God wrestling.' I said, 'He's mine and you can't have him.' God responded kindly, yet insistently: 'He's mine and he's on loan to you, like everyone else.'"

Edie Weinstein, Reverend

"Death, like a prairie fire, is a promise of renewal."

Kyle Garcia, Marketing director, gallery owner

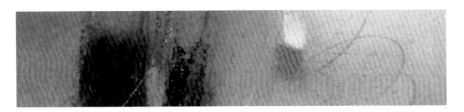

"I don't know that I can say what death is, but I do have a story that illustrates what death means to me. I call it my Easter story.

I was raised in a foster home by parents who were two generations older than me. They adopted me when I was six and cared for me as best they could. By the time I was 11, I had outgrown them in many ways.

In December 1993, my 81-year-old father suffered a stroke. The last time I saw him was Christmas Day. He was the buffer between my mother and me, and he was always trying to make peace.

Shortly after he died I received a letter from one of my cousins who is a generation older than me. She expressed regret at not intervening during my growing up. She also told me some things that showed how my father was as much involved in my childhood isolation as my mother was.

I entered therapy in 1994 as part of my work on family issues. I took workshops and did some journaling that included working with dreams. I was in a creative writing program and my thesis included poetry based on my relationship with my parents.

Relations with my mom deteriorated. The last time I saw her was Christmas, 1995. In 2000 I moved and I didn't give her my new address. Even though I still had dreams reliving the dysfunctional family dynamic, I felt I put that part of my life behind me. Eventually I stopped dreaming about my parents. In 2006, I got rid of my books and CDs, except for a few that resonated with me. I went through papers I had saved and got rid of them. I felt I was starting a new chapter and I needed to trust that everything I needed was within me.

I came across my cousin's letter and re-read it. I was surprised to find that I had completely forgiven my parents. There was no bitterness, anger or pity — just love and acceptance. The following year I occasionally dreamed about my parents. In these dreams all was harmonious.

On Easter Monday, 2009, I was walking a labyrinth with a couple from my church. We went to dinner afterwards, and they asked me where I was from and about my family. Given my family history I make mental calculations about just how much I'll tell people. This time I told them everything. I also told them that my adoptive mother was dead, although I didn't know this for certain. When I got home I reflected on why I told them she passed away. I came to the conclusion that given who she was, and who I was, we could only come to forgiveness after she died.

I went online, searched my hometown newspaper and found her obituary. She died in 2003 at the age of 87 — two and a half years before I experienced our forgiveness. This story is the best answer I have to 'What is death.'"

Gigi Ross, Spiritual director

"About a month after my father passed away, my mother said, 'Your father appeared and started talking to me.' It was the first of many visits in the weeks after his burial. She said these weren't dreams — that he was right there with her — asking how she's doing, and even comforting her when she cried and complained that she didn't know how to do certain things on her own. She said he encouraged her to go on with her life.

One night he came and told her he wanted my mother to commission a Sefer Torah, a handwritten sacred scroll that's placed in the holiest part of the synagogue. To have one dedicated to you is a mitzvah — a good deed.

A torah has to meet strict standards; it takes many months to complete and it's expensive. They can cost up to $30,000. My mother had a fight with my father and said, 'Are you crazy? How can I afford that?' He said, 'Don't worry, I have an account in the bank.' He told her the name of the banker and said, 'Go see this woman, she will find the money for you.'

My mother knew the bank well. She had accounts there. She couldn't believe there was an account she didn't know about and a banker she'd never heard of. She was embarrassed to go there and ask, but she eventually did. Sure enough, this banker told her of a special account my father had, and made it available to my mother. There was just enough money to pay for the creation of the Torah.

The phenomenon is that as soon as she went to the bank the visits stopped. Months later, we gave a beautiful new Torah to the synagogue. At the dedication celebration, she raised a glass to my father and said, 'Well you asked me to do this...and I did!'

We had a hard time believing it back then, but, to this day, my mother swears that these weren't dreams, but live visits from my father."

Shlomo Ben-Hamoo, Real estate broker

"Death is the ultimate freedom: no more pain; no more sorrow; no more cares. It is the end of all you are and will ever be.

Waiting for pie in the sky by and by may help some cope with life. When all is said and done, though, death is just the end of existence."

J. P. Leghorn, Retired

"I am hoping that death is just the stopping of the physical body. I believe that people you loved and met in the past are there to welcome you when you cross over.

I have seen a few people pass and it seems that this is what happens. I have multiple sclerosis and I believe that I will be in a better place and with those that cared about me."

Gina Benner, Substitute teacher

✿

"I look at death as being the end of this chapter on earth. It's obviously inevitable and it's sometimes far, far too soon.

When you lose somebody really close to you, the only way I can possibly understand coping with that grief is to constantly remember and relive the memories of that person. Although it's a deeply painful loss, I feel grateful to have had that person in my life.

Sweeping their memory under the carpet isn't for me. I try very hard to discard the 'what if' thoughts. I feel, or hope, that those loved ones who have gone before us are still with us some or all of the rest of the way and that perhaps we shall all be reunited in some afterlife."

Hailey Dart, Founding Director,
Rodwell Dart Memorial Foundation

"Uh, say what? I am not so presumptuous as to even begin to contemplate what death is. I do know it isn't worthy of capitalization. I'm not looking forward too much to extinguishing my consciousness. However, I think that there is probably (sorry Jesus, only probably) something after death. But whether or not that is self-awareness or reincarnation, God forbid, I would not want to do all this over again. Whether or not that is on a human/personal level with all emotions you had alive intact, or whether or not you ascend or descend, as the case may be, to a different plane, I have not the faintest idea.

I would probably love to have some sort of afterlife consciousness so that I could see what happens to my children and grandchildren, or be able to have dialogue with my spouse forever, since she is a very good conversationalist and a smartie. But I don't think I'll be floating around on a cloud playing a harp and wearing a white robe. I don't look good in white because I am a slob. My ex-sister-in-law can play the harp, and she's very good at it so I would have to take a backseat."

Hal Weiner, Licensed New York City sightseeing guide, journalist

"I am not afraid of death, I just don't want to be there when it happens."

Woody Allen

"Death is nothing at all.
I have only slipped away to the next room.
I am I and you are you.
Whatever we were to each other,
That, we still are.

Call me by my old familiar name.
Speak to me in the easy way
which you always used.
Put no difference into your tone.
Wear no forced air of solemnity or sorrow.

Laugh as we always laughed
at the little jokes we enjoyed together.
Play, smile, think of me. Pray for me.
Let my name be ever the household word
that it always was.
Let it be spoken without effect.
Without the trace of a shadow on it.

Life means all that it ever meant.
It is the same that it ever was.
There is absolute unbroken continuity.
Why should I be out of mind
because I am out of sight?

I am but waiting for you.
For an interval.
Somewhere. Very near.
Just around the corner.

All is well."

Henry Scott Holland,
Professor of Divinity, University of Oxford, 1910

"We as a human race begin dying at the moment of life. To answer what is death, one must answer what is life.

Experiences in life define what death will mean to each person. Helping one person through a difficult time with death; whether it's for themselves or a loved one, is in a way holding one's hand as a friend when in need.

The only thing in life that we take with us in the end is the memory of holding one's hand. If you have never witnessed death, it is not what you see on television. It's an emotion that demands respect and honor.

If you demand respect and honor, then hold someone's hand. The reward you will receive is better than anything you've ever dreamed of, because respect and honor is earned."

Hattie Lord, Hospice Advantage team coordinator

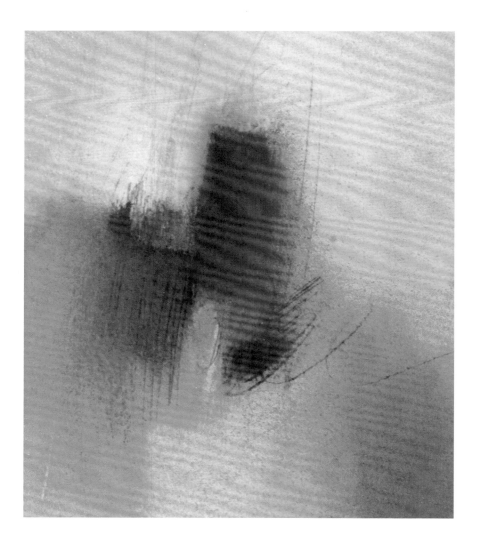

"The passage between this world and the collective unconscious, along with birth, is the ultimate transformation for human beings. It's definitely not an end of life, but rather a transition between this lifetime and the next."

Hilary Harley, Writer, astrologer

"Death is a process of transformation.
Depending on one's individual culture, the transformation will develop. This topic is very vast...but fascinating."

Ileana Guelbenzu-Davis, Doctor in philosophy

"When you become an octogenarian you know that you are nearing the end of life as most know it. For me, it has been a matter of getting my affairs in order and making sure that my family is taken care of when I'm gone.
Simply put, death is the end of life."

Anonymous

"Death is birth backwards."

Jenny Lynn, Photo artist

"'Life does not die.' (Chandogya Upanishad V1: 11.3)

Life changes and is not taken away. Residency is not always on this plane. There is a very thin veil between this side, the phenomenal world, and the other side, our temporary paradise until we reincarnate again.

While on this earthly plane we have the opportunity to realize the Inner Spark of our Divine Self. To do so we must pass through our small, ego-driven self. As we heighten awareness of our ego in action we can self-observe and see our conditioned state of mind in action. A purifying experience, to say the least. What a grace-filled challenge. Is this a Death? Is there suffering? Only if we do not see the action of the Divine Will.

In surrendering to the Divine Will everything becomes exquisitely perfect."

Joan Tonyan, Director of health care center

"Everyone dies. We are the only animal species which understands that at some point we will die. However, in our culture death may be seen by a physician as being his failure.

We say, 'He passed away.' No one passes away — they die. We say, in the medical field, 'The patient expired.' We are a culture that avoids and denies the reality of death.

Studies show that the greatest fear of most dying patients is not that of losing their functional abilities and control, but of pain.

Pain, however, is defined as physical, emotional, social and financial. All of these need to be addressed with a dying patient in order to help alleviate or lessen pain.

Unfortunately, we don't do this. When I worked in hospice, I had a patient, Tommy, who told me that he was sure that he was dying and going to Heaven. He also said that he was sure that when I died, I would go to Heaven and then he would take me out for a lobster dinner. I have a happy memory of him because he could be open about his dying.

I think that it's very important for those of us who are dealing with the dying process of a loved one or a friend or a patient to be emotionally available to that person and to be able to give dignity, recognition and understanding to that person."

Jane Herron, Created hospice programs around the country

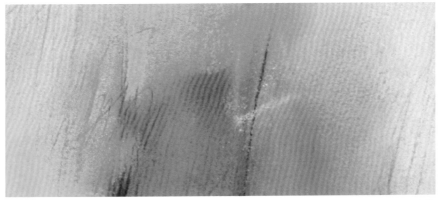

"Our culture has a very difficult time dealing with death and dying. Many times people just give up on eating, and families will continue to push fluids and food when their loved one doesn't want it. Society feels that if we don't eat we will die, but really it's the other way around. We have stopped eating because we are dying."

Jody Holeman, Registered nurse

"I can't remember a day in my life when I didn't talk to my father. When he died at the age of 90, I thought it would be the saddest day of my life. But I was wrong.

I realized that he had given me his all, and there was nothing more to give or share. I felt fulfilled and relieved. I was happy. I don't remember him as frail, but as he was when he still had his swagger, till the moment of his last breath."

John Slotkin, Owner, health care family assets

"Death is an illusion, the unappreciated gift with its grand certainty. Death is demanding our participation — sooner or later, and always eventually."

Jolee Henry, LPC, Psychotherapist

"Your soul leaves your body and your spirit is free. A hospital where I grew up would open the hospital window and let the soul free whenever someone would die.

The soul and spirit continues to surround us with their love and care for their loved ones. My father and some close friends died, and I can feel their spirits around me. They became guardian angels.

In February, 2004 I was at meeting in my office and reached over for the phone. I was on a rolling office chair with no arms. As I pushed myself and reached for the phone, I fell so hard on a ceramic and concrete floor that I broke my earring.

A few days later, I felt strange and I went to the doctor. I couldn't remember where I was going. The doctor ordered a CAT scan and it came back abnormal. He ordered an MRI and they found a brain tumor. My father had a malignant brain tumor, but mine wasn't. I believe that because I had no prior symptoms and could have started having seizures that my dad pushed me off of that chair. My dad experienced very bad seizures and would fall to the ground.

Because, my dad's brain tumor was malignant and there wasn't as much medical knowledge in the '80s of brain surgery as there is now, he turned out like a vegetable. Needless to say, when I had to have brain surgery I was totally petrified — but I had to or things would have become worse.

My surgery was successful and I am able to lead a full and normal life. I believe in angels. (I also consider my neurosurgeon an angel.)"

Karen Lee Hirst, Advertising sales representative

"Death is a dissolution of the physical body, leaving your essence to float into the universe, where it adds to the general beingness of the planet. The sum total of what you have done then becomes part of the general energetics of the universe.

I would like to believe that I can be a physical being in another, parallel world and reunite with loved ones. But I don't think this is possible. I have been putting forth effort to contribute to the positive energies. I am holding on to each experience as much as possible, and have spent much time honing the ability to be 'present' to cull the most out of my moments on this earth.

It is slightly overwhelming to think of not being here in this manifestation, as I enjoy life so much and rue the passing of the years. As a result, I am staying as alive as possible and shall do so until the day something happens to take me from this presentation.

I do wish that people wouldn't have to suffer with disease, poverty and misery."

Dr. Judy Kuriansky, Psychologist, TV and
radio commentator, author, humanitarian

"Death is but a doorway to a new destination where the body is shed and the soul can soar."

Laurie Sue Brockway, Interfaith minister, author, editor

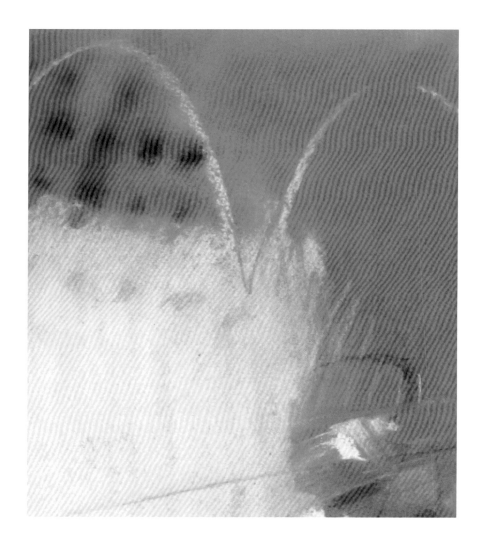

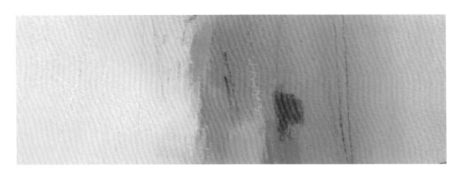

"Death is the soul inhabiting the body for a short time, just 'the blink of an eyelash.'

I have survived cancer two times and I've had six surgeries. Each time, a close family member — my father, my husband, a friend — has asked, 'We're going to see you afterward, right?' And my answer was, 'I'm going to do the best I can.'

Each time my body was very sick. All of its resources, its immune system were fighting to restore health, but the illness was very insidious. But I am still here and I was victorious.

For me, death, is a transition of the soul. It may be born into another body immediately or after awhile. This part I do not know. But what I do know is that my personality, my ego, the 'I' will not pass on. These are part of the body and the mind and will not pass on. The soul and the spirit are eternal and will go on forever.

I also know that I am not afraid of death. The only thing that I wish is that I don't have pain and that I don't end up with my mind gone and my body housed in a nursing home. I hope my transition is easy and peaceful and I hope to die in my sleep. Is God involved? Yes I do believe in God as a universal force. I don't anthropomorphize God into a man, a person or an entity. So I really can't tell you if God is involved in death since I believe that the life of the soul is eternal and only the body and mind will die. I keep in contact with the sanctity of life by practicing Reiki every day and in many different ways. For me Reiki is like a continual prayer. It keeps me connected to the universal energy, the force that keeps the 'me' that is my mind, my body and my soul alive."

Jacqueline Rose Thrope, Artist, Reiki master

"I define death as absolute stillness and total surrender.

It is a state of grace with no struggle, where we recognize our true nature and fully connect as one in the ocean of life rather than as a single drop of water, separate from the other drops.

I have the ability to contact and receive messages from the non-physical. I asked George Harrison on the day that he died, 'You knew you were seriously ill and you have followed a spiritual path. What was this experience like for you?'

His answer rang true: 'Karen, I was unprepared for the unspeakable joy.'"

Karen Lee, Reiki master practitioner, CHT

"In the past year, I've lost my cousin, my stepbrother, my aunt/godmother and my mother.

Death is absolutely a loss. No getting around that. People like to sugarcoat the loss or try and make you feel better by saying, 'Oh, she's in a better place.' Or 'She's not suffering anymore.' There's truth in that, but really those statements are from the dead person's perspective, aren't they?

I do believe that, as the law says, energy cannot be created nor destroyed. We are all energy. Standing by my mother's hospital bed as she passed away in that moment, we felt a huge, enormous surge of energy leave her body. The room became electric. Then the energy was gone and she was gone. I believe her energy has gone somewhere else. I don't know where. Perhaps into many other things.

For days after she died, I became obsessed with asking others what happens when people die. I heard the religious points of view (heaven and hell), I heard the new age points of view (we return to the earth), I heard complicated answers and I heard agnostic answers (it's like going to sleep).

All I know is that to us who are still alive, death is a loss. I miss my mother terribly. So terribly it hurts. I feel that society doesn't like us to see death as a loss. And I don't understand why. It's as though the unknown is so scary that we tell ourselves all sorts of things to cope with the unknown.

My mother had cancer and suffered in her last year alive. She was ready to die and so was at peace with it. She used to say to us, 'Don't pray for my speedy recovery, pray for my speedy exit.' So while I see her death as a loss, to her, it was not a loss. It was a triumph over suffering.

I'm not afraid of death. It's the idea of the loss associated with death. In thinking about my own death, I fear the loss of my loved ones: my siblings, my dog, my friends. I fear the loss of not swimming in the ocean or walking in the forest."

Jennifer Repo, Book editor

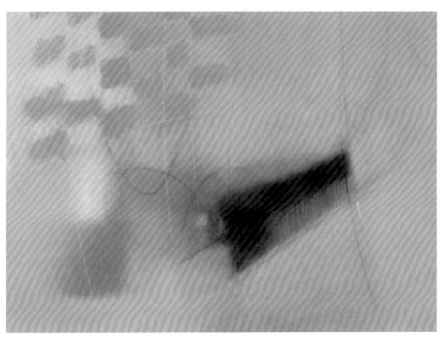

"Death is the end of our body as we know it. The moment of death, the last breath, is peaceful. Dying, the process to death, can be rough.

The process of letting go into the unknown, having pain, having fears, knowing a violent end — these can make dying a place that most of us fight, deny and hope to avoid. How can we prepare to die?

J.K Rowling, in her *Harry Potter* books, says, 'Death is but the next great adventure.' If we are energy, then even after death, we are still essence in an altered form of energy. We become like the wind and the air we breathe. We can not see them, but they are still there."

Karen Andrews

"For me, death will be the end of something wonderful, but also the beginning of a fantastic journey.

I don't need the answers to life. Everything I need to know I find in the smile of my daughter's eyes. I have faith that the answers will be revealed in death, making death not something to be feared, but to be comforted by.

Death is there, somewhere down the line. The most important thing about death is reminding me that today, this very day, I should live life completely and enjoy time with my family and friends as fully as possible."

Kenneth W. Bledsoe, Manager, fine art photographic printing

"Death is the other side of life, a constant companion/guide — the other side of the coin. Death is the kiss between two consciousnesses. Karl Jung wrote, 'Death is a drawing together of two worlds, not an end. We are the bridge.'

In the gypsy culture, at one's death the troupe stops and everyone wails for days. Our culture so needs a model for dying and grief."

Kay Moates, Artisan

"Three years ago both of my parents passed within three months of each other. It was a rather metaphysical experience. The things I saw could have only come from an ethereal source or altered nature. Our society doesn't like to speak of this. Those who have not experienced it become uncomfortable.

Can we dwell in the physical and spiritual simultaneously without considering it a requiem? I suspect if our society were more open to and respectful of our senses, we would know the benefits. The one thing I found consistent in both of my parents' passings was the sense of calm they had when they were surrounded by love. "

Lisa Kane Jung, RN, Video producer

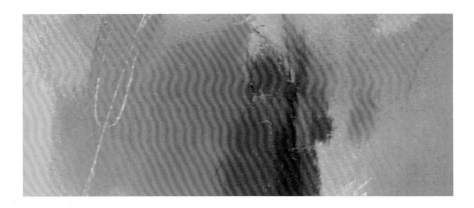

"Death is that state that follows life. It is on a continuum that follows this life.

I believe in an eternal soul and glorified body that continue to be united after earthly death. I believe this as a matter of faith, but the concept is almost beyond human conception. I do not believe that what we perceive as death is the end. I have lost many close people in my life and often at too young an age. It is hard, but I believe the living have to go on living."

John J. Trause, Library director

"I believe that when you die you go to another dimension. You will see your friends and family who have passed before you.

With just a thought you will be where you want to be, see who you want to see and you will experience whatever you believe you will experience.

Death will be just what you make it, just as life is what you make it. It is just another experience in the path we have been traveling. We chose the path. We chose the people we needed to be around to learn something we needed to learn.

If we want to see God, then we will. If we believe we will go to hell, then we will. We will still do things that are important to us. If we choose, we may be angels who help the living. We may help people pass over. We will be able to watch over our loved ones still here.

The most important things in our lives are our relationships, and they will continue. The knowledge we gather here will help us in the next dimension. We will have our own life review. We will judge ourselves instead of being judged by the almighty. We will experience the feelings we caused people here in life to feel and then we will know. We will see the good we did and the bad we did.

We will be met by loved ones to help us cross over."

Jennifer, Nursing student

⚘

"I believe that death is freedom. Freedom from the physical body, which has been my vessel in this lifetime. A freedom like no other, where my soul can fly and soar!"

Kristal Hardy, Caregiver

"Death is slipping out of our physical body on this earth to the heavenly body that has been in store for us all along. We are a shell on this earth with a beautiful heavenly body and soul inside.

In illness and natural death we slow down. We become quiet, need less nourishment and less physical activity. I believe we are reflecting on our lives and need less stimulation. Families and loved ones don't handle this well, as they don't want their loved one to slip away. I really believe this unresponsive or coma-like state is necessary to the patient to complete their journey. Most of the time, death is peaceful, although sometimes it isn't. I really think that depends on your station in life, your faith and your acceptance of death and your loved ones' willingness to let you make this final journey.

Death is as natural as being born. We have no control as to the timing or the circumstances. As far as accidental and/or sudden death, I have to believe there is still a window of time for the individual to reflect and to be able to choose eternity. Although it may not be apparent to us as family, emergency workers or medical workers, our heavenly father wants us all in eternity with him. That has always been the master plan."

Mary Beth Raymond, Registered nurse

"I don't believe there is a death. I believe we carry on."

Pat Hickman, Cantor, rabbi

"Death is love's best friend. They intrinsically intertwine in death's loving embrace. Difficult it can be to open our eyes and see beyond the physical world of death where forms seemingly disappear each day. The Buddhistic beauty of emptiness is form and form is emptiness. Or in the words of Rumi: 'Each form you see has its unseen archetype. If the form is transient, its essence is eternal. If you have known beauty in a face or wisdom in a word, let this counsel your heart: what perishes is not real.'

These words light my fire. Every day I see death in the invisible world around us. As they say in Hinduism, sacrifice is the nature of the universe and when we participate willingly, we form ever deeper, more intimate connections to what the Native Americans call the spirit that moves through all things. The I-Thou relationship analyzed in Martin Buber's mystical judaic writings is perhaps the closest thing we have to analyzing the love-death partnership. But I turn to my Christian roots for a definition of love that causes me to sing.

Love is an exchange, a continual receiving and accepting, giving and releasing. It's a continual process taking in everything that is given to us fully and then releasing it fully back into the world. The Rev. Cynthia Bourgeault said it's 'constantly renewed intimacy.' The gap between the giver and receiver grows ever narrower through ongoing exchange until it ceases to exist and we are one.

What does that look like when we love the divine? Each time we give up a piece of ourselves to that which is greater than us, a small death happens inside and around us, but in its place is an ever wider channel for love to flow through us. And so the intrinsic nature of love and death."

Kymberly Kline, Community organizer, environmental scientist

☙

"The American poet Walt Whitman contends that death is the natural continuation of life.

I, however, am hard-pressed to subscribe happily to this theory. One feels sorrow and grief with the loss of a loved one. It takes time to heal and move on.

Death is the absence of life. It is a void. It is the blank stare left after the soul departs. And yet, after the grieving and sorrow subsides a bit, there comes the realization that death offers the unique opportunity to carry on the work or mission of loved ones. In doing so, their spirit and love live on. It lives on in our actions, our thoughts and our love.

Our souls aren't divided by death, but rather reunited and transformed."

Kelly G. Lavis, Teacher

☙

"It's the end of the beginning."

Lis Kalogris, Consultant

"Death occurs when the physical body dies and the soul is released and returns to whence we all came. I'm not exactly sure where or what this is, but I'm positive it exists.

I believe people continue to do the work they started here. I have had the opportunity to meet with two different channelers. One was accidental. I was at a spa and it turned out that the owner was a channeler. He invited several of us to join him one evening. He told me things about my brother who had recently passed over that surprised me. He told me about his physical state (he had an illness), and why he chose to leave.

For years my friends figured I was just grieving so much that I had to believe this. However, many years later, while working on an article as an editor at a New York City newspaper, I encountered a second channeler. I took my mother to meet him, and remarkably he started describing every family member who had crossed over. These are people I vaguely remembered as a child. He described each them to a 'T.'

I had a little test this time. If my brother was real and still alive he'd mention the camp we went to. Sure enough, my grandmother, my aunt, my uncle, my great-uncles and my grandfather on my father's side were all there — each vying for attention — with my grandmother dominating the conversation. My brother wasn't there. But boy, were the other family members real. My aunt, who had died shortly before we saw the channeler, showed up first. When we asked how she was, she said, 'Look, we're together again,' triumphantly raising the hand she was holding of the man she was with.

The channeler accurately described my mother's brother and my aunt's first husband who had died 40 years earlier. Finally, my mom and I said we were disappointed that my brother didn't come. The channeler said he'd try to reach him. And finally he showed up. He explained about the work he was performing in the 'halls of knowledge' and then he mentioned an old bunkmate from Camp Sequoia."

Kathy Bishop, Editorial and content director

"Death is the process for spiritual beings to leave their physical bodies and complete their current life on earth. It is the path back to God, and it is a beautiful completion for their current incarnation.

The spirit and soul are freed from the limitation and restriction of the physical body. Albert Einstein proved that energy cannot be created or destroyed; it merely changes form. So the spirit and soul cannot die. It simply changes form by leaving the physical body."

Lee W. Papier, Life coach, wealth advisor

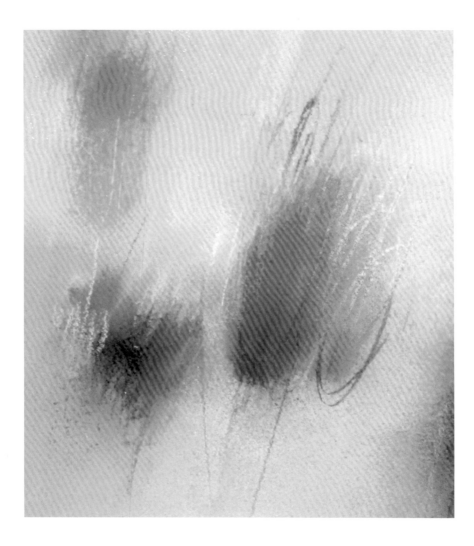

"As a small child I can remember feeling that there has to be more than one lifetime that a soul must travel in order to learn all there is in the universe.

Humans have so much to learn that it would be incredibly sad if we only had a short time here on earth. Although I was raised Lutheran, my belief system is a mixture of cultures, religions and life experiences. I believe we have a final destination, call it heaven or nirvana. I believe that we have many lifetimes to get it right, and that death is only a transition to the next learning experience.

I had a very vivid dream one night that my mother came to check on me. What was so extraordinary about this dream was the fact that my mom was a teenager, full of life and joy. She was very much still my mother, checking on me and making sure I was taking care of myself, but in an altered form.

After losing many friends and family over the years, I still feel their presence with me every day. Some may say that is just wishful thinking that our loved ones stay with us, but I know in my heart that they are still with me everyday."

Lori Pederson, Founder, ididnotknowwhattosay.com

"I believe that I am here to ascend spiritually, and that my sole purpose now is to bring more light, love and God's guidance into my life."

Meredith Porte, Producer/host, public television

"As we journey into this world, each birth is unique. As we journey from this world, each death is unique.

Although death is the end of our journey on this earth, it is the beginning of a new life, yet again, unique.

Death is simply a transition from one life to the next."

Lisa Chappell, Administrator, registered nurse

"We are exquisitely crafted instruments of Creation, designed for constant change and impermanence. The cells with which we awakened this morning will morph into something else by the time we retire. And even though our bodies will eventually disintegrate and decay, our spirits will emancipate and move on.

This is the law of the Universe, which is constantly supporting our soul's deepest desire to expand and grow into the best version of ourselves. If we can greet each day with a personal inquiry on how to maximize each moment as a growth experience — regardless of our apparent local reality — we can then peacefully put our heads on the pillow at night while whispering our prayers of gratitude.

As we focus our attention on being aware of the rich treasures that are certain to ripen our awakening hearts through each breath experienced fully, we can then become more and more enthusiastic for the joys and mysteries of a life beyond — willingly ready to surrender our body-temples."

Luann Robinson Hull, Clinical social worker

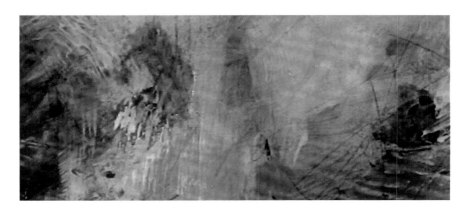

"Energy can neither be created nor destroyed. It can only be transformed from one form to the other. Energy or life force or soul inhabits my physical body at the moment. Only the body dies, while life cannot cease to exist.

Life, or *Jeevatma*, leaves the body to occupy another after it has lived to its fullest, and unites with the *Paramatma*, God or the Universe. Hence there is no need to fear death.

What we all actually fear is the inability to continue our physical association with all the material attachments that mortal life has to offer, which manifests itself as fear of death itself. A little bit of introspection and reflection will free us from this fear.

All religious and spiritual practices help us detach ourselves from the material aspects of life and embrace bliss as long as our physical body exists."

Mahesh Mohanan, Founder, saranam.com

"Everything has a shadow. Night is the shadow of day. Winter is the shadow of summer. Sickness is the shadow of health. Old age, the shadow of youth. And death is the shadow of life.

The shadow is not the opposite of the light. A world without shadows would seem very flat and lifeless indeed. A life without shadows would be shallow, superficial and false. It is only because of the shadows that we can see the wholeness, the three-dimensionality, the complex completeness — of which the dark is a part of the world around us.

If it were not for the shadows, we could not appreciate the light. It is the contrast which illuminates. Life is light. And life is dark. If we only strive for the light we are living halfway. We lose half of every day. Half of the year. Half of the full spectrum of our feelings. Half of our lives. And there are just some things that you can only learn in the dark.

The dark offers invaluable lessons, which give us a chance for enlightenment. Death teaches us to live life. To be consciously appreciative of each day, each hour, each minute. To engage ourselves passionately in all that life has to offer. The good, the bad and the ugly. For better or for worse, for richer or for poorer, in sickness and in health, till death due us part.

This is the ultimate lesson of death."

Mama Donna Henes, Urban Shaman,
certified funeral celebrant, treeoflifefunerals.com

"I view death as a transition from experiencing this earthly journey.

Our body is like a garment we get to wear and use as an instrument to carry our personal energy field, which is our true essence. What we call death is when the garment, or its parts wear out.

We do not die. Our life force moves on. The fear of death is mostly related to the unknown. There is not as much fear surrounding the transition for those whose belief of death is similar to mine. I had a Hermetic teacher who used the term 'graduation.' I have grown fond of looking at the transition that way. It is very difficult to part with a loved one. For love is a very strong emotion. I do feel it is important for family and friends to realize you have not lost that person, but now have a different relationship with them. They are still around you. Very likely they are guiding you.

For those of you that are open and accepting, they will also visit with you and communicate with you. It is only fear that is fatal."

Marla Phillips, Minister of healing

"Death is the end. Death has no meaning except to those who aren't dead. To them death is what you call the thing that happened to someone they knew, who isn't knowable anymore, because their life ended.

There is no reason to expect there to be anything after, or during, death from the dying person's point of view. It all comes down to childish fear, and the ridiculous expectation that there must be an answer to the question, 'Why would we have sentience, if it is only to have it end?'

As I say to my religious friends; if there's an afterlife, cool; but what if there isn't? That's just as likely from a probability perspective, and slightly more likely, if you factor in burden of proof. So the question begs: If you live your life based on the constraints of a given religion, you risk not getting everything out of it that you could have. If you live as if this is all you are going to get, you at least have the chance to get everything out of life that you want. Which is a more rational way to frame your existence?"

Marc Aniballi, Generalist

"What we call death is simply the end-point of one cycle involved with the material realm. Think of a guitar string. When plucked, it goes back and forth between two nodal points crossing the mid-point each time. When the string finally becomes still, it is at rest.

Life consists of not only one but many strings vibrating to ever-changing chords. Death is when the strings settle down and exist simply as potential waiting to once again be plucked.

What chord combinations will you play?"

Michael Thau, Nonprofit reforestation

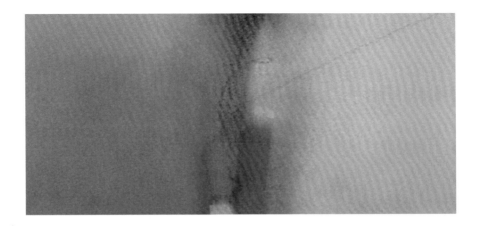

"From a Jewish perspective, death is nothing to be afraid of. Death is the next leg of our journey. What's most referred to as death, is really a transition between life and life. We transfer into the next world, or into paradise, a Garden of Eden, as in home of souls.

The transition of going from a spiritual world into the physical world is hard for the soul, so we may think that it would be delighted to return home, back with fellow souls and G-d. But once it enters the body, it sees the opportunity it has to transform the world, and leaving the body takes away that opportunity to change the world, to have an impact; so it has pain. Hence the pain associated with death. Not only do we physically miss a loved one or a friend, but they physically can no longer have an impact.

A story that illustrates this point is that of the great Talmudic sage Rabbi Meir and his wife Beruria. Their two children suffered from an illness and died. Beruria brought them to their bedroom and covered them with a sheet. Rabbi Meir arrived home and asked about his children. After avoiding the question, she responded, 'My dear husband, I have a question. A man came and left an item for safekeeping. I really like the item; do I have to return it?' Rabbi Meir replied: 'Is it not the law that a custodian is required to return the deposit to its master?' She then took her husband's hand and led him to the bedroom, where he saw his two children lying dead. Rabbi Meir could no longer contain himself and broke down in tears at the loss of his two children. Beruria comforted him, saying, 'G-d gave us the two precious treasurers to safeguard. Now G-d has asked for his items to be returned.' This, I believe, is a beautiful way to look at our souls and the process of death.

G-d trusted us with something, and gave it to us for only a certain amount of time. Until death, the soul was able to make deposits into its eternity account; now it can only make withdrawals.

G-d gave every human something special on loan, but at a time not of our choosing he asks that it be returned. So death is not bad, it's real sad. From the soul's perspective, it can't accomplish anything anymore. From the human perspective, we miss our loved ones. But death is not a negative. It's a transition, and transitions are not easy.

How we live our lives here on earth affects and makes the transition easier, as that is a source of comfort for those left behind to carry the torch going forward."

Mendel Mintz, Rabbi

"Death begins when we are born into this earthly realm, which gradually becomes a rebirth into eternal life. It is an ongoing process of living and dying as we evolve in stages from a state of sleep into a state of awakening at each level of our spiritual transformation.

It is a journey of returning to the Source of our essential being in an awakened state of consciousness. Throughout the duration of our earthly existence we are offered experiences specific to our evolutionary capabilities.

Our consciousness progressively awakens and expands in preparation for our arrival at a state of recognizing our true identity: our Oneness with the Divine Architect of our being and all other sentient beings. 'Unless a kernel of wheat falls to the ground and dies, it remains only a single seed. But if it dies, it produces many seeds.' (Jn. 12-24) In other words, we remain in a temporal world of phenomena, which is experienced as separateness and aloneness.

When we allow that 'seed of understanding' to be transformed through dissolution and death, then the Light of Life itself breaks through to reveal the unity of consciousness which connects all life forms as one.

Death, in its most profound meaning, is an experience of transitioning from our earthly form into the formless state of ultimate reality, where we experience our oneness in the web of life versus our separateness in the phenomenon of life."

Mary Regina Hudak, Movement therapist

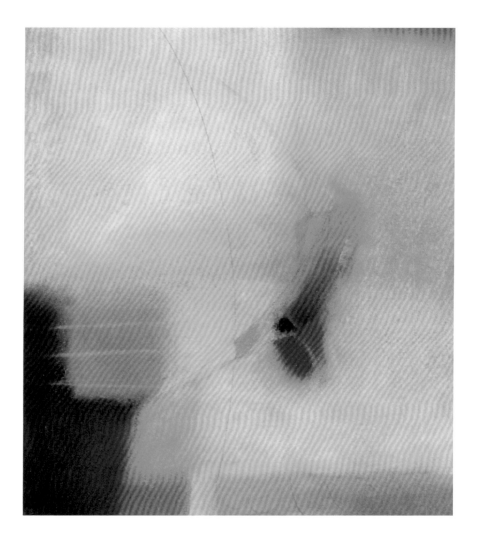

"A brother's death.

On a personality, level my brother and I were not very close. Our life paths, and the consequential perspectives on life we accrued from those paths, made it challenging to connect with each other beyond a superficial level. Sometimes months would go by before either of us communicated. The distance between us wasn't so much in miles but in our attached concepts of who we thought ourselves and each other to be.

I had known for over a year that he was having some challenges with his finances and health, and that he seemed down. I didn't know that nine months earlier he had been taken to the hospital by his daughter and admitted into the psychiatric ward. He was eventually diagnosed as clinically depressed and with borderline paranoia. When I received the call from my sister that he had killed himself, it was an unexpected shock. The fact that he hung himself was particularly disturbing.

Each person has their own response or reaction to death. For myself, despite religious conditioning, the 'issue' of death is not resolved. Perhaps this is only fitting as the 'issue' of life should not be resolved, either, but deeply explored.

There is a part of me that does not fear death at all, that recognizes it as part of the larger tapestry of life and knows that some kind of continuance after physical death does exist. Most of humanity calls this the domain of soul or spirit. Yet there have been times when my own mortality, either through intense psychological stress or potential physical harm, has suddenly erupted into my conscious awareness, and there was indeed the presence of fear within the disturbance. That fear I knew was on a deep level related to death. We are so conditioned to identify with the body that the fear of losing relationship to it is understandable. The longer I live the more I recognize the importance of opening my heart to the mystery of death, with respect, with compassion, with honesty and on really good days with humor.

After my brother's passing there were three events that solidified my recognition of and appreciation for the levels of communication and healing that can occur after someone physically dies.

First, I was concerned with the 'state' of my brother's consciousness on the other side, having died through suicide. I had moved beyond the 'all suicides will burn in hell' dogma that I had been earlier indoctrinated with. Yet from my spiritual studies there was a concern about his possible distorted mental and emotional state at the time of death along with his choice to 'opt out' of life's lessons, so I was worried about his being lost or trapped in an area of the bardo, or intermediate state, that would make it difficult to move into the higher realms of light. As the intelligence and grace of life would have it, a friend mentioned to me a particular type of group process that might be of benefit for my own healing regarding my brother's death and might even assist him, as well.

We met in a room that had 12 paintings hanging on the walls — with one painting being on a wall by itself. My brother was a loner, pretty much his whole life. While I was being interviewed about his story the painting hanging on the wall by itself crashed to the floor. The potency of that moment was not lost on any of us. There was a moment where another person, whom I had chosen to play my brother, was laying on the floor, as if dead, and I said something about how I wish I had communicated in a way that could have helped. The other person lifted his head off the floor, looked directly at me and said, 'There was nothing you could have done, it's not your fault, it's no one's fault.' There was something about the way he said it that was as if my brother spoke those words. I burst into tears, not only from the release of unacknowl-

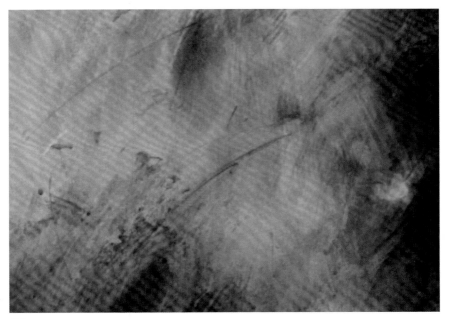

edged guilt, but more from a deep awareness of how much I really loved my brother. I have no doubt that somehow the group process facilitated this communication between my brother and I for mutual healing.

A week later, a respected lama was coming to an ashram in New York to present a healing sound ceremony with a group of monks. There was an invitation for participants to bring pictures of loved ones to place on the altar so that emanations from the healing ceremony could also be extended to them. I asked the lama's assistant if I could place my brother's picture on the altar. I was disappointed to learn only living persons' pictures could be placed upon the altar for this specific ceremony. I explained the situation of my brother's death and the assistant asked, 'Has it been a month or longer since his death?' I said it had been 29 days ago to this day. He excused himself to speak with the lama and asked me to check in with him again after the lunch break. The lama, who didn't speak English, was informed of my brother's death. Because it hadn't been a full month since his passing the lama agreed to take my brother's picture. He said he and the monks would do a private puja, or worship for him at sunrise the following day.

This was indeed an expression of the hand of grace touching my life, my brother's life, and offering the balm of healing capable of permeating the veil of death."

Michael Edan, Holistic health practitioner, energy healer

"Death is a transition. When younger people pass I tend to feel that they are chosen in a sense — that their work is done here and they are needed somewhere else.

My sense is that death is freeing. The body and both the collective unconscious and consciousness are dense and heavy on the being. I feel that death frees one from those levels of denseness.

I believe that we are incarnated from loving energy matter into the physical body. We come from Divine Unity and will eventually return to Divine Unity, but the body holds the opportunity for a different kind of evolution.

We are in constant forward motion whether we like it or not. When the body/being has served its purpose here, the spirit and soul continue on its path of forward progression."

Maria Tafuri, Licensed marriage and family therapist

"I've heard death described as, *merely the extinguishing of the candle because the dawn has come* — a definition that points to death as a passage from one realm of existence to another.

This definition also indicates that death is a part of life itself and not some unnatural interruption or cessation of being. Some Native American groups speak of death as a natural flow. They describe *death happening to him* as opposed to the statement *he or she died* — as if death is an act wholly and completely in the hands of the person who is dying.

Death is an almost incomprehensible experience — mysterious and mystical yet carrying aspects of the raw, radical and ancient. It is the shifting and reshaping of energy — the spiritual life force that fills and directs all living things. Death is uncommonly common — an ordinary experience in the sense that it is common to all, yet becomes uncommon or extraordinary when faced by a single individual or family.

Perhaps my response to 'What is Death?' may be summed up in the simply profound declaration: 'Death is life.'"

Mark Hundley, Licensed professional counselor

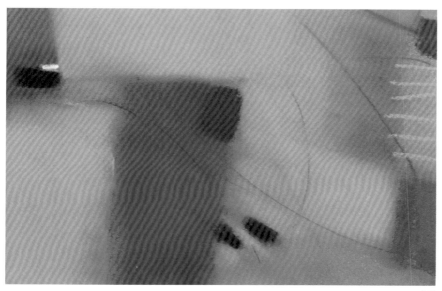

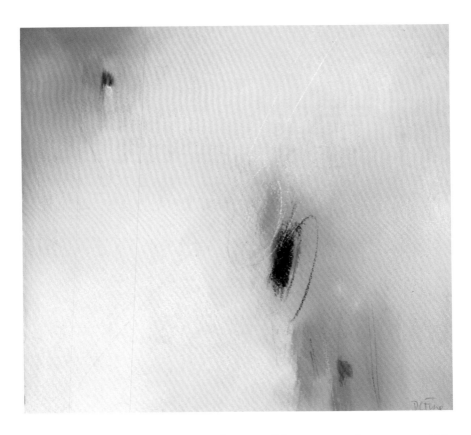

"I believe that death is a change of form — nothing more. We let go of the physical body and become non-physical. I believe that the 'energy' or 'life force' that truly defines a person can be transformed but not destroyed.

Emmanuel said that death is like taking off a tight shoe. That has always made sense to me. I've lost quite a lot of people in the last few years. My friend Keith died of AIDS at the age of 29. He was probably the funniest person I've ever known. I remember feeling his presence shortly after his death and thinking to myself, why would he be here with me when his mother might need him with her? I immediately heard the following in my mind: 'I can be in so many places at once now.'

A few years later I went to see a psychic. There were about 40 people in the room, and each of us was instructed to write down our full name, followed by the full names of two deceased people we wanted to contact, followed by a question we wanted to ask them. We were told to fold the papers in half, and they were all placed in a basket together. He then put masking tape and a blindfold over his eyes. He took each piece of paper out of the basket individually and crumpled it in his fist. He said the name of each person in the room. He mentioned Keith and said, 'He walks with you.' It was the most remarkable psychic reading I'd ever experienced.

When my mother died, for a period of about two weeks a mourning dove visited me outside my window no matter what time I got out of bed. If I got up at 8 a.m., the mourning dove was there. By 11 a.m. it would gone. If I got up another morning at 11, the mourning dove was there. It felt like a message from my mother."

Melanie Votaw, Freelance writer

"Death is the end of your assignment on earth. We have lessons to learn and gifts to provide. In the first part of life, we are busy trying to figure out what those gifts are and how we can provide these gifts to the world.

The second part of life, once we discover these gifts, we question them. In the third part of life you give your gifts. If you're a woman you've been programmed to give and you sometimes find yourself totally burned out. If you've been on a spiritual path and you're able to give, you know how to protect yourself from being burned out.

Pure giving starts in the last part of life. You bless others and you know that it is a blessing to be alive. Death is where you recharge so you can go back to earth to learn more lessons and provide lessons for others."

Myreah Mia Moore, CEO, True Colors Productions

"Death remains the vast black hole of human biology.

We cannot know its contents with any certainty. But the black hole isn't *just* black. The uncertainty over what death holds creates an opportunity.

In the absence of actionable information, each of us, individually, is free to imagine what we'll find there: Angels. Old friends. Deceased loved ones. Oblivion. The terminus of termini. The obliteration of all possible beginnings.

In this respect, I think, death becomes the ultimate repository of all our wishes and expectations — a black hole filled by our minds with whatever fits our constitution. Hope. Or the end of hopes."

Steve Volk, Author, *Fringe-ology: How I Tried to Explain Away the Unexplainable — and Couldn't*

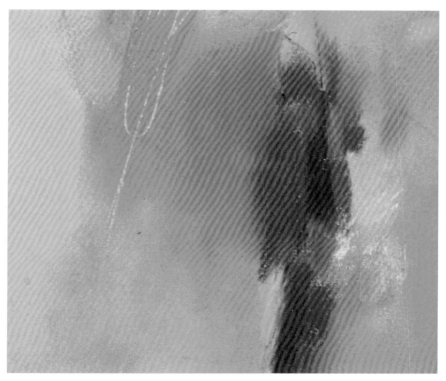

"In order to understand what is death, we must first understand what is life. To me, life is the soul acting as a kind of electromagnetic force. It forms an apex in the great void, drawing together all the surrounding energies necessary to satisfy its unique makeup until it becomes manifest as physical. Thus, this unique soul is able to interact with other unique souls — manifesting in physical, emotional, psychic, intellectual and spiritual ways. Such is life.

Death is simply the soul releasing its electromagnetic charge, dissolving its physical manifestation and returning to its unity with the source of being.

Death is the soul returning home."

Moshe Sussman, Licensed massage therapist

"On the final day of my father's life he came out of a short coma he had been in and 'spoke to each of us' with his eyes. He tried to speak with his voice but was unable to.

I went home to bed and was awoken by small flashes of light similar to flashes of static electricity. I woke my husband to show him some sort of unusual electric current in the room. As it ended, one of my sisters came by to let us know Daddy had died and that we had to make arrangements."

Molly Terlevich, Political fundraiser, philanthropist

"A friend asked me, 'What do you think you will be like after death? I mean, what is your view of the nature of the afterlife?' I replied, 'I think I will be just like I was before I was born.'

'Oh, so you think you existed before birth?'

I asked him, 'What is the definition of eternity?' Its not just without end — it's without beginning. I'm not the physical body, or the mind or thought or feelings; the real 'I' isn't limited to such a small parameter. The real 'I' is something both at the very core of being and beyond the limits of the physical world.

Death is just a cessation of the physical, mental and sensational realm that I experience now. The real 'I' was, is and will continue to be existence beyond comprehension."

Orion Pitts, Spiritual seeker

"Death is nothing more and nothing less than a step in our personal evolution as we continue to move and grow towards greater wholeness and a more perfect union with all that is.

The return to the source of our being at the end of our earthly journey is simply a change of form as we are transmuted back into spirit to continue to refine our essence in the subtler realms of existence, taking with us the imprint of all that we have learned and all that we have loved in this world."

Dr. Patricia Hill, Television producer/host,
author, *Becoming Whole Again*

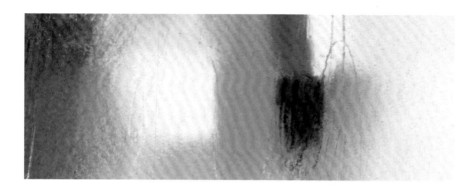

"Having now lost my mother, my aunt — who was my 'second' mother — my father and my daughter, I feel I know a lot about death. I don't fear it. I believe that death is a transition out of the burdens of flesh into the lightness of pure-energy being.

I had the privilege and honor to birth and bury the same person, my beloved daughter Holliday, who left this physical human life plane at age 36 in 2004. She died of a horrible illness, HIV/AIDS, and left behind the legacy of truth, that living with HIV/AIDS, with its debilitating effects on mind and body, was far worse than ending it all in silence and going beyond the pain through passage into death.

As her mother, I remain dedicated to eradicating this horrific disease spectrum by offering sex-positive information, education, counseling and marketing messages for this totally preventable pandemic. Holliday left behind a daughter, my granddaughter, whose life is my new focus.

What is death? Having witnessed the transition, and it indeed is such, it strikes me that leaving the human life form is a heroic, mystical and profound experience. It is a moment of heightened awareness for the beholder, but more than that, it can be felt as an energy shift.

It is a holy moment. It is awe-inspiring. It is a final frontier for us as humans to know, embrace and accept. I wish others to know about from my own, personal, ravishingly wondrous (though grief-stricken) experience in holding the hand of my daughter as she took her literal last breath and was gone.

I am told that hearing is the last of our bodily senses. The highest gift we can give the dying one are words of encouragement for the soul to leave the physical realm: 'It's okay,' 'You may go now,' 'I'll be fine.' Death is a gateway to another realm of being and knowing.

I strongly feel that. My friend died and came back on the operating table and shared her soothing words with me that death is not the final destination at all. Allowing death to be a partner at our side gives us life at its fullest.

I honor death and know that when my time comes, it will be a positive, powerful and peaceful, evolved state of energetic being where I go.

May we all dare to embrace death as a part of life itself. I miss my daughter, yet I know she is truly in a better place where she is free. Blessed Be."

Patti Britton, Sexologist, sex coach, professor, author, speaker, healer

95

"I experienced death when I was only eighteen years old.

My family and doctors told me that I was dead for about five minutes. Those few moments felt endless. I left my physical body. Another body just like mine — more fragile and flexible — elevated. I could see myself looking in.

What was strange was when doctors tried to bring me back to life; I watched everything that happened with total calmness. All of a sudden, I felt an energy force similar to a vacuum that sucked me inside a tunnel with a lot of speed. I had no control at that moment. I lost all calmness. I felt fear, but not for myself. I was feeling the fear for my father and sisters. My mother had passed away a few years earlier.

I started to scream and pray for them. I didn't want to leave them because they needed me. At least I felt that way. This came from my heart with a lot of agony. Suddenly, the journey through the tunnel ended; I saw my self alone and in total silence. I had a feeling of becoming small as if I were wearing a leaf from a big tree that falls to the ground far and away.

Suddenly, I started to see a light that took over me completely. The light got bigger and brighter and there was a silhouette behind it. I couldn't see who it was. I felt a lot of peace and a lot of love.

I can't describe by words how I felt. I communicated with the light by telepathic form because my mouth was never open. The energy force gave me instructions that, to this day I still try to remember — but only the end was in my memory. I was allowed to come back because I was told that I had cared about others and that I did help and serve others in selfless ways.

At the time I was too young and didn't value that experience with enough deepness, but through the years I learned to value the gift of life. Life is eternal after the physical death. It doesn't matter if scientists deny it.

I know now there is life after death and we become eternal!"

Sandra Levine, Hair stylist

&

"Death is the only thing in life that is permanent.

It is scary and surreal simultaneously. It has forced me to confront my questions about spirituality and afterlife. I was 31 when my father died at the age of 62, and his death has changed me in many ways.

The death of a family friend at the young age of 15, just two weeks shy of her 16th birthday, has made my belief in G-d even more questionable.

The most difficult part of death for me personally is the ability to speak and see and touch and love someone one day and then having that all taken away the next day. With that said, I feel the presence of the two great losses in my life more vividly than when they were present on this earth and for that I am grateful."

Randi Goetke, Special educator,
developmental evaluator, family trainer

"I have no idea what death is, but, to paraphrase Supreme Court Justice Potter Stewart's comment on pornography, I'll know it when I see it."

Merna Popper, Writer, art dealer

🍂

"Once you are done with your 'job' here on earth, it's time to go home. He will send for you."

Patsy Greene

🍂

"I believe that death is the completion of a journey. I believe that we all experience many journeys through many lifetimes, and that with each journey we learn the lessons that are necessary for us to exist in the subsequent lifetimes.

There are times when we might find that something we're experiencing is or sounds familiar. These experiences, feelings or thoughts are a result of having already experienced them as previous lessons or occurrences in previous lives.

As we journey forward through time, we will eventually find our last journey — a journey of blissful peace as a result of having fully evolved intellectually, emotionally and spiritually."

Rev. Raquel Algarin, Holistic nurse, interfaith minister

"As thought by many, love never dies. Therefore, when a person dies the love is carried with them in their souls forever.

Death to me has always been a distressing and devastating part of life. I choose to never think about it as it relates to a loved one as it is something unfathomable to me. If a person has lived a long, happy, healthy, fulfilled life, it is easier to accept.

We will always remember the love we share with someone long after death."

Tara Elias Schuchts, Real estate

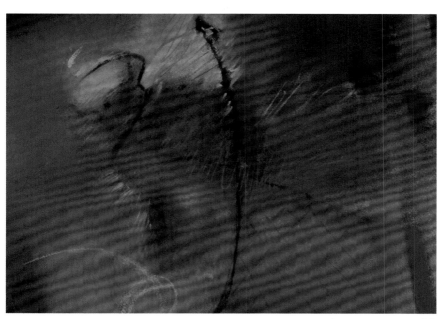

"Death is when our souls leave most of the constraints of the physical world and gradually become closer and closer to G-d for an infinity of time. Each step of closeness bringing us more and more pleasure. We've earned this closeness through the good choices we've made in the present world.

Upon death, souls appreciate more fully the implications of their thoughts, words and actions by seeing a much bigger picture. All souls rejoin in reviewing each person's life. Good choices are relived. Sorrow occurs in the face of those who didn't make good choices. If the dead have touched people in a good way in this world there will be additional pleasure in the world to come. The more we love everyone in this world in thought, speech and action, the more pleasure we get in the next world.

Adolph Hitler was evil, yet he considered himself to be a good man. Imagine reaching him as a young man and touching his soul with love so maybe, just maybe, he would have dwelled on love instead of hate."

Ra'anan Elozory, English teacher, videographer, editor

"Death is life's equivalent of turning off the light and entering another room. Just hope the other room isn't the basement."

Robert Bruce, Television writer

"Death has been different for me through the stages of my life. I remember my grandmother on my dad's side passing away when I was a teen. I wasn't that familiar with my grandmother and it didn't phase me much. I knew everyone in the family was upset and I was upset because I knew that I would no longer get to know her.

I have known many people that have passed away as clients with my job. As a nurse, you tend to keep everyone at arm's length. You miss them and remember many of the good things. I have lots of great memories and have known so many good people that I would not have known had I not been a nurse.

My father passed away when I was in my 40's. It didn't happen overnight but I remember thinking, this is it. There is no God because if there was he would have healed my dad. It was a reality shocker. I always thought that God fixes and prevents things from happening to people you love.

I gradually got my faith back and then, after a couple of years of struggling with my son, I lost him to suicide. This has been devastating. I felt denial, guilt and at times I really wanted to die. I questioned God. What did I ever do to deserve this and why me and why my son?

It's taken time but the best I can figure is that maybe God did save him from whatever misery he was going through.

Death is letting go of the person you love and hanging on to the memories, whether they are good or bad. They are memories."

Sherry A. Graham, Vocational nurse

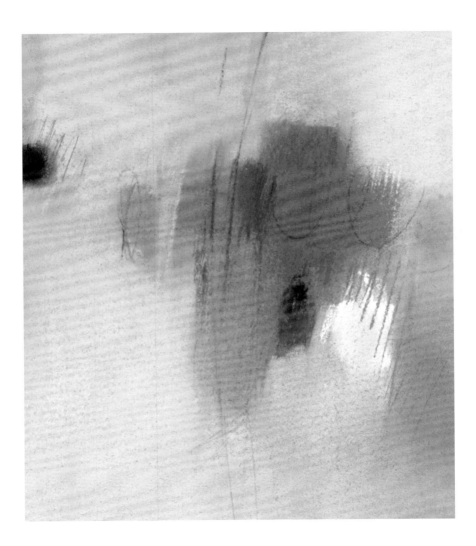

"Death is a dream-squasher. Everything you long for in life is trod upon — snuffed out like a candle flame — when death comes knocking.

In that sense death is a sad reality. However, if you're one of the lucky ones who believes in the hereafter or reincarnation, death takes on a whole new meaning. It's not so final — it's just another step in the cycle of life.

I'd like to believe I'm going to get a second chance — the chance to do everything I wanted but didn't have the time or courage to even try. As I get older I think to myself, 'You better stop messing around. Stop being lazy, stop being petty. Time's a-wasting. You're not invincible, you know. You're not bullet-proof.'

Or am I? No matter what you believe about death, the thought of death should be like a whiff of smelling salts. It should stimulate you to start living — living like there's no tomorrow. It should arouse your creative juices — yes, we all have them.

Believe that you are an eternal soul. Believe that love is eternal — then death is life."

Roberta Miller, childrens' book author, dog walker/pet sitter

"The great use of life is to spend it for something that will outlast it."

William James

"To me death is like a portal to another world, whether it be Heaven, Hell, or whatever it is a person chooses to call it.

I believe that the physical pain ends at death and not the spirit or energy of a person. The body dies but the spirit lives on.

Within the past few years my grandmother and my mother died. It was very devastating to me. My mother was my role model and probably my absolute very best friend. I am glad to know she is no longer in pain. My mother and grandmother both had cancer.

From my experience 'Mom' was dancing, laughing and having a good time after her earthly body died. My dreams and experiences afterwards gave me great comfort. I do not believe death itself hurts, or causes pain. What causes the death may. I also believe that there are angels all around us working and helping us, and that we all have 'spirit guides' or 'angels' with us at all times to help us through our times of grief. Thank God!"

Sabrina Lynd-Hurt, Mother

"Death is when the body ceases functioning, at which point we can't prove what happens to our consciousness.

At that point we have access to experiences of all lifetimes, all sorts of dimensions of being that living in a body prevents us from being cognizant of.

But, of course, I can't prove it."

Stephanie Gunning, Publishing consultant

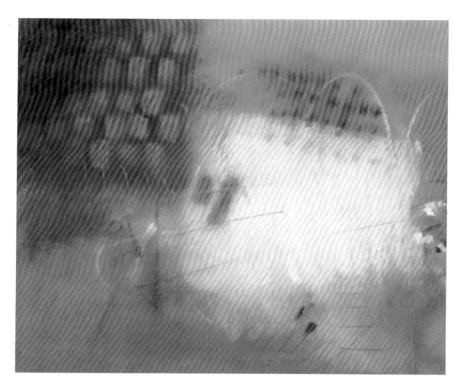

"When my grandpa died I missed him so much. He went into a cocoon. We planted him in sand and soil. Then, my grandma came from heaven as a really big, beautiful butterfly of golden light and brought grandpa, also a butterfly of light, back with her to that wonderful place."

Sonya Maya Tralins, Age 5

105

"To paraphrase Carly Simon, death is a horizon we can't see beyond because of the limits of our sight.

I've had medium-ship experiences in which I heard the voices of people who have passed on. Sometimes these voices have been so loud that I'd whirl around to see if anyone was behind me. I've also had the experience of having psychic friends give me messages from people in my life who have passed on.

Psychic communication knows no bounds. We live on many planes or dimensions all at once. Quantum physicists tell us there are ten dimensions, but that we are aware of only three. When we leave this three-dimensional reality, we will see beyond the horizon — we will open to a dimension or dimensions that have been hidden from us because of the limits of our sight."

Sorah Dubitsky, Teacher

"When humans die our bodies live on with our spirit, which is in the image of God.

I remember vividly when I walked into the hospital room of my just-departed 25-year-old brother. He had been in a motorcycle accident 35 long days earlier. I stood by his bed, waiting to talk to someone, anyone, who could tell me what happened and what would happen from here. He was so small, so empty, so vanished, so absent from his body that I hadn't realized for a few minutes that his remains were still in the bed under the sheet. The nurse came in and asked me if I would like to see him. I felt the overwhelming need to see his face again, one last time. But my reaction surprised me. When I was 10 years old, I had fallen to the floor upon seeing my dear grandmother in the casket. But somehow I was joyously relieved when I saw my brother. As I looked down at his withered facial features and pale skin, I chuckled through my substantial tears. Which took the nurse by surprise after I shouted, 'That's not my brother!' A smile formed on my wet face as the nurse looked at me, confused. I realized his reaction and assured him that there was no mistake, but that Gary was no longer there. I knew that he was no longer with me and that his body was an empty vessel. The lack of life presence was strong. This truly helped me at the time to start mourning his loss.

Death is the absence or release of life's force, energy and abilities. What made a person who they are is no longer there. They have left us. The life force has moved on to exist elsewhere.

Thank God that we will be reunited again one day."

Sue Bulos, Mother, author

"At the moment of death, our body reveals itself as the womb it has been all along, and what has been quietly growing within it throughout the course of our earthly journey — the realized meaning of our existence — is finally ready to be born."

Rev. Cynthia Bourgeault, PhD,
Teacher of Christian contemplative wisdom and practice

"Shiloh was my only child. On June 2, 1992, at 1:20 a.m., I fell asleep at the wheel and 'My Best Kid' — that is what I sometimes called her — 20 years old, was killed.

What is Death? Shiloh and I talked about what each of us thought, and it was our opinion we just went back to be the God we came from. She knew that death was not to be feared. She accepted as truth that when she was done here on Earth, she would leave. She wanted her ashes spread in the mountains.

I miss her each day and when I think of her, I see the smile she almost always had and hear the laughter she voiced often.

I remember the fun we had backpacking, skiing, traveling and laughing with each other. I killed my daughter and I am 100 percent responsible for her death. I live with this knowledge. Yet I live my life to the fullest and each day I work at being the best and happiest person I can be. I do this because I know she would not want me to feel guilty, be unhappy or dwell in remorse. She sometimes called me 'My Best Dad.'

My father never spoke about death. Ever. When Shiloh met death, my father opened up about it, wrote a living will, gave power of attorney and told us he wanted his ashes spread on the mountain where he lived.

Months after Shiloh died I was in a deep meditation, and she came to me. I said, 'Shiloh, I killed you,' and she replied, 'No. You didn't.'

In another meditation, she said, 'Dad, I am a higher God now.'

Eight days before she died, she asked a good friend if she

knew how she was going to die. This friend said she did not and asked Shiloh why she asked. Shiloh said because she knew she would die in an automobile accident.

Twelve days before she died, she told her Mother that if she should die 'in an automobile accident or something,' she wanted to be cremated and her ashes spread in the mountains.

Shiloh's ashes were given to Lake Manasarovar, at the base of Mount Kailas, in Tibet.

Her life was filled with love, peace and laughter. As a child she was unconditionally loved and was encouraged to find her own way. She and I had read *The Prophet* by Gibran, in particular 'On Children,' and we knew this was how we were with each other. We said I love you to each other every day. We hugged a lot. We left nothing unsaid. When Shiloh met death, we were complete with each other.

It was my privilege to be a Father for 20 years with 'My Best Kid.' And Death cannot take that away."

TJ Krest, Builder

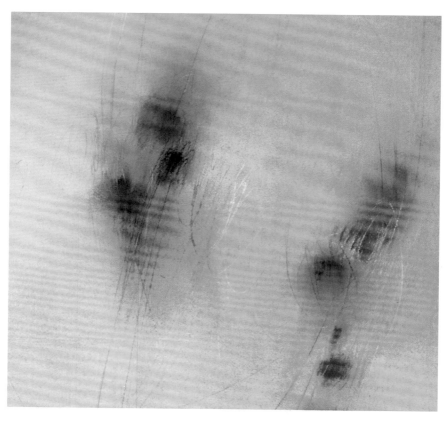

"I can't picture death in any special images. I do believe in life after death and that is in the form of a spirit. I believe death to be a spiritual environment and a gathering of our loved ones that have passed.

The feeling of calm and love would be my guess, at some unknown place where we would be happy. There have been many passings in my family over the years, including my beloved son who died at a young age of 39. I feel his presence often and even know that he continues to watch over us. I frequently feel him at times when something is missing or some kind of joke that only he would have done when he was alive occurs. This continues, even twelve years since he passed away.

There are many feelings and dreams that occur not only with my son, but with my mother, father, brothers and sisters where I definitely know that they continue to watch over me. When it appears that I am in a desperate situation, they come to my rescue.

I was the youngest of eight children and there are only three of us left. The strongest contacts have been my mother, my oldest sister and my son. On occasion I have actually felt their presence. There are times when I smell roses when there aren't any in the house or in bloom. Roses and lilly of the valley were my mother's favorite flowers. I have a strong belief in God and pray to him each night and thank God for letting me have and live the joy of my family — living and dead. When my time is due I expect to join my family once again in God's presence.

Before my son died, I lived in constant fear of dying and fear of what I would be once I died. Now, I no longer fear dying, although for my family that is still living I want to stay on earth as long as I can."

William Canham, Consultant

"When I was a little girl I thought about death all the time. It was all around me. My parents and both sets of grandparents had survived the Holocaust and their barely restrained whispers about the traumatic events they endured followed me wherever I went.

Virtually every day of the year, memorial candles were lit for dead relatives and on Friday nights, Sabbath candles were lit for the living and also for those who died in the war. Our table literally looked like an inferno.

I grew up in a very Hasidic family where there was a promise of eternal reward, peace, freedom and joy in death. Of course, one had to live a life free from sin, full of good deeds and follow the Torah faithfully. Death happened to everyone and if you were a good little girl or boy, the afterlife was the ultimate reward. Living and the process of dying was much harder! I had to list all my sins before I fell asleep in an exercise called *Cheshbon Hanefesh*, literally, the counting of the soul so that if I died before I woke up from my sleep, I would be transferred immediately to Heaven and bypass the fearful hell we called *Gehennom*. I continue to recount my sins nightly — just in case.

I knew death was not absence of life because all the older living relatives spoke of the dead ones as if they were there, merely resting in another room or away on vacation. They were mentioned at every sort of family gathering (The Bubba Malka is here!) and we would turn our heads and see if we could see her. We made bets that she would indeed show up one day.

My grandparents and other relatives who passed away did not

die at home but in hospitals, tethered to machines, robbed of their dignity in their last moments. I thought of death as an ending for their suffering but also as a new beginning. We do not know what lies on the other side and some people go to their death with frightened and contorted faces and others with a peaceful smile.

I am known to say that when a baby is born, the baby is crying and the family is smiling. A good death is when the individual dying is smiling and the family is crying. I am not frightened of death — it is a merely a destination to an exotic place that I haven't yet discovered. I only hope the journey there is a peaceful one."

Tobi Ash, Midwife and critical care nurse

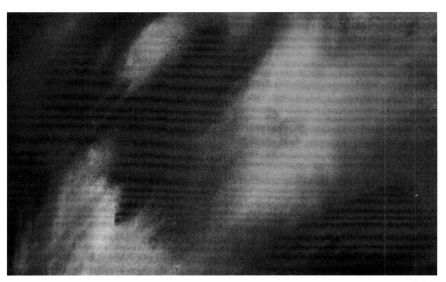

"Animals have these advantages over man: they never hear the clock strike, they die without any idea of death, they have no theologians to instruct them, their last moments are not disturbed by unwelcome and unpleasant ceremonies, their funerals cost them nothing, and no one starts lawsuits over their wills."

Voltaire

"Death is the end of one's journey and the beginning of another.

It is the release of one's soul to a higher place. As my family gathered around our dying mother it was apparent that she was ready to end her journey here on earth and begin her journey to a different place.

She left us with such grace and the faith in what was waiting for her.

We were not ready for her journey here on earth to end, but as the hospice nurse told my daughter and I, 'She was there when you took your first breath, the least you can do is honor her by being there when she takes her last breath.' Such a profound moment of witnessing death.

Bodily she was gone but her soul lives on. She had the easy part. We who were left behind have the hard part — continuing our journey without her.

Death takes us when it is our time to end the journey, whether it is all of a sudden or through a long, painful process. I believe death can be a test of our faith. A faith in a higher being.

Is there one? Or not?"

Terri Giesken Guzman, Medical front desk specialist

"Death alleviates our sense of impermanence. It allows a greater clarity than we experience now because fear of death is destroyed, and we are all equal.

Death finds us with many more answers than questions and the grace we need to find the remaining answers. Beyond death is hope and insight. These do not disappear when we journey across the boundary of earthly knowledge.

Death is luminescent; from here, it looks like a magic trick that fails, where people disappear and don't come back to sparkles and celebratory music. Now, and especially in times of grief, we abhor death for its separation.

Only past death will true spiritual query lead to true spiritual understanding. Reality does not prepare us for death. We continue to be surprised by it, taken off guard. We are spooked by death, stifled by fear of it, but time will teach us that death can be trusted.

Death is the umbilical cord for eternity, a virgin birth, a welcome sent from beyond our time that says with zeal: 'Come and rest for a bit, then we'll celebrate.'"

Tamara Miles Gantt, English teacher

"Elizabeth Swados answered the question musically: 'The tears of the living; the thief of a man.' People don't die; only their bodies do.

In physics we know that energy cannot be destroyed, only converted to another form. Death breaks the bond between consciousness/soul and the body, releasing the spiritual being into the non-corporeal realm to carry on in that new form. Without physical eyes, spirit beings can probably see the front and back of an object at the same time.

Well, so much for playing poker. I imagine they'd have multidimensional games instead, which I cannot fathom but are probably lots of fun. I'm sure my mom's kickin' up a storm in the next world and paintin' the town red — whatever their equivalent of a town might be — so I try not to pester those in the spirit world. I just hope that the time domain is less an issue for them so that when I do call on one, it won't be too much of an interruption. Maybe without a physical body they are better multitaskers.

I don't know if reincarnation exists, but I definitely don't believe in transmigration — coming back as a 'lower' form of life. Being a Gemini I can argue both for and against reincarnation. I once had a memory of a past life, which makes me believe it; but there is also the possibility that while the memory may be real, it also may not be my own and simply wafted into my brain from the *Akashic* records and just felt like it was mine.

In any case, life continues some way, somehow, somewhere, in this elegant universe."

Walter Ian Kaye, Inventor

"Funny you asked. I am dying. I have been diagnosed with and living with a rare, incurable cancer for the past five years.

At this point in time, I have exhausted all the known approved treatments plus a couple of experimental trials. The tumors in my abdomen are now growing out of control with nothing 'they' can do. I am quickly moving toward my last days on earth, to be preceded by a medical crisis.

It is very difficult as I have so much to live for with seven grandchildren who are close in proximity and heart to me.

I believe in God, our creator, and Jesus, the triune, father, son and holy ghost. Death is as natural as birth and should be celebrated. We as humans just tend to be scared of the unknown, as death is the ultimate unknown.

I do believe that loved ones who preceded us come for us at the moment our heart stops beating and our souls leave our bodies to escort us to heaven.

What is heaven? Beautiful and peaceful — not of worldly thoughts. I can't tell you any more. I have faith that when we leave this earth behind our souls live in peace and harmony.

Does this mean I am never scared? I am, sometimes. More about how I will pass. This is a very painful cancer. I have struggled these past months with evil trying to enter into my life and thoughts. I literally say out loud 'devil be gone — you cannot have my soul — that belongs to God.'

I do get mad occasionally. Obviously having started my family at a very young age I feel as if I deserve to see how it all turns out. We would be egocentric to think 'this' is it — our time on Earth. There is sooo much more that awaits us."

Wendy Warren, Human services program coordinator

"Death is the beginning."

Sonya Nance Rodriguez, Mother, wife

"It is the perpetual movement of life, passing from one paradigm to another. It is the blessing that we are given at the end of our current life, once our physical body has decided to expire.
I see golden white light in our future."

Dave Jensen, Doctor of chiropractic medicine

"I realized that it's insane to oppose it. When I argue with reality, I lose — but only 100 percent of the time."

Byron Katie, from *Loving What Is*

"Graduation."

Michelle Hill, Sports and fitness copywriter

119

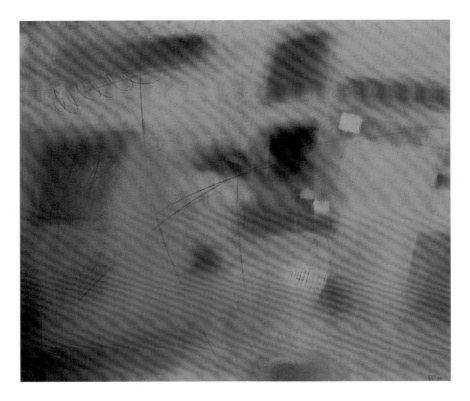

It takes me by surprise.

There, at the footbridge
Over the darkened water,
I hear it–the faint tinkling
Of glass.

Clear notes carried
On the west wind.
It is the lake ice.
Once thick but now,
After several days of warming sun,
Reduced to shards
That glint faintly in the dim light
Of shrouded moon.
Tomorrow, they will be gone,
Melted into the depths
Of the lake.
But tonight,
Tonight,
I am graced by their singing.
And so my wish is born:
That when I am called to surrender
To my Source,
To say my "Yes."
When my self is broken
Into a thousand shards
And I'm lifted by the waves of love
To the shore,
May I, too, make music.

Maryjude Hoeffel, *On the Path to Emmaus*

How Different Religions and Classic Thinkers View Death

Hinduism

"There is no death, only a change in worlds. Though death seems to most of us a fearsome and unfamiliar affair, we are constantly being educated in its ways, for life is a continual process of change, and each change is a little death survived. Not only do we live encircled by death, but to live is itself to die: From the moment of birth, each breath we take inexorably draws our death nearer. Nevertheless, despite its constant proximity, death for most us is the mightiest of challenges..."

The Upanishads

"When a person here is deceasing, his voice goes into his mind; his mind into his breath; his breath into heat the heat into the highest divinity."

The Chandogya Upanishad

"This is how the death experience will be: When one practices good actions, one can die peacefully. At the moment of death, wealth, good positions, husbands, wives and possessions do not mean anything. No matter how much we have, we all leave this world empty of materiality. Worldly wealth has no meaning at this moment, only inner wealth. Divine wealth takes us to the divine. Depending on how we have spent our life, we will experience one of two paths: one is light, beauty, joy, contentment and merging with divinity; one is non-light, based in fear."

Sai Maa Lakshmi Devi, Founder, Humanity for Unity

Buddhism

According to Buddhism, it is important to train ourselves right now so that we can die well. When our vital functions cease, the gross level of consciousness dissolves and the subtle consciousness, which does not depend on a physical support, manifests and offers a unique opportunity to the seasoned practitioner to progress towards enlightenment. That is why, particularly in the Tantras, *one finds many meditation methods aimed at preparing the practitioner for the moment of death.*

"Death is a part of all our lives. Whether we like it or not, it is bound to happen. Instead of avoiding thinking about it, it is better to understand its meaning. We all have the same body, the same human flesh, and therefore we will all die. There is a big difference, of course, between natural death and accidental death, but basically death will come sooner or later. If from the beginning your attitude is 'Yes, death is a part of our lives,' then it may be easier to face."

Dalai Lama

"What is death? Death is the cessation of the connection between our mind and our body. Most people believe that death takes place when the heart stops beating; but this does not mean that the person has died, because his subtle mind may still remain in his body. Death occurs when the subtle consciousness finally leaves the body to go to the next life. Our body is like a guesthouse and our mind like the guest; when we die our mind has to leave this body and enter the body of our next rebirth, like a guest leaving one guesthouse and travelling to another."

Kadampa Buddhism, Death-and-Dying.org

Tibetan Buddhism

"Central to the Tibetan concept of after-life existence is the *Bardo*. The word means literally 'intermediate state'... the *Bardo Thodel* describes a distinct sequence of states (bardos) through which the individual passes through between death and rebirth. There are three distinct stages.

1. The *Chikai Bardo*. Intermediate period of the moment of death. This includes the process of dying; and the dissolution of the elements (Earth, water, fire, and air) that make up the physical body.

2. The *Chonyid Bardo*. Intermediate period of visions of deities.

3. The *Sidpa Bardo*. Intermediate period of rebirth. During this bardo the consciousness descends and chooses a new body to be born into."

M. Alan Kazlev, from *The Tibetan Afterlife* (*Tibetan Book of Death*) — "The 'Bardo' Or Intermediate State"

Judaism

"The Jewish tradition teaches that death does not end a soul's existence. Life — our essence, our spirit — survives the failure of the flesh. Rather, death represents a transition from one state of consciousness to another level of consciousness — a disembodied spiritual awareness. After bodily death, a person's immortal soul enters several non-material realms where it undergoes a series of transformational experiences designed to help purify it and consolidate the lessons of the life just lived. Life after death thus represents an evolutionary journey of consciousness consisting of various stages of learning accompanied by an integration of the experiences from the deceased's immediate past life."

Lewis D. Solomon, *The Jewish Book of the Living and the Dying*

"While death represents the soul's elevation to a higher level, it nevertheless remains a painful experience for the survivors. At the same time, it must serve — as must all experiences in life — as a lesson. We must see death not as a negative force, but as an opportunity for growth. The Sages teach us that it would be barbaric not to mourn at all, but that we should not mourn longer than necessary. To diminish our expression of grief is unhealthy and inappropriate, but to allow our grief to overwhelm us is to selfishly overlook the true meaning of death — the fact that a righteous person's soul has found an even more righteous home."

Rabbi Simon Jacobson, Jewish Learning Institute: Soul Quest: The Journey Through Life, Death, and Beyond.

Islam

"The experience of death is rather like that of a man who has lived all his life in a dark room and suddenly finds himself transported to a mountaintop; there his gaze would embrace all the wide landscape; the works of men would seem insignificant to him. It is thus that the soul torn from the Earth and from the body perceived the inexhaustible diversity of things and the incommensurable abysses of the worlds which contain them; the first time it sees itself in the universal context...and takes account of the fact that life had been an instant, but a play."

Fithjof Schuon, Understanding Islam

Christianity

"A classical Christian perspective on death typically refers to the life, death and resurrection of Jesus. The Gospel of John is often quoted: 'For God so loved the world that he gave his only Son, that whoever believes in him should not perish but have eternal life.' In the Epistle in Romans we read: 'For if we have been united with Christ in a death like his, we shall certainly be united with him in a resurrection like his.' Yet, the subject of death and life after death has always been part of everyone's human story since the beginning of history. And this Christian emphasis is not necessarily the story of Jesus, but rather the storytellers of Jesus after Jesus' death.

Professor Marcus Borg expresses concern with the overemphasis of the Christian afterlife as it distracts from the more essential teachings of Jesus. It can also be divisive, creating distinctions between the believers and non-believers, righteous and the unrighteous. Borg also reminds us that 'there is nothing in the Lord's Prayer asking that God take us to heaven when we die. Rather it is stated, 'Thy kingdom come, Thy will be done on earth as it is in heaven.'"

Marcus Borg states that as a committed Christian he is an agnostic about the afterlife and clarifies agnostic precisely as one who simply does not know for certain. Then he states, 'What I do affirm is very simply: when we die, we do not die into nothingness, but we die into God.' In other words of the apostle Paul: 'We live unto the Lord and we die unto the Lord.' So whether we live or die, we are the Lord's. For me, that is enough."

Gregg Anderson, Minister, Aspen Chapel

"The story of Mary Magdalene really begins at the moment of Jesus' physical death, and its epicenter is always the profound transition point between dying and awakening to a new reality. The difference between the two streams is that for canonical gospels (at least in their orthodox interpretation) Jesus returns from the dead to a fully resuscitated human body. In the wisdom stream, by contrast, Mary Magdalene is the one who crosses over, and their meeting takes place in the imaginative realm. It may also be unfolding simultaneously in the physical realm, but in any case this is not the main point. Her recognition of him is not simply a raw human response to a stupendous miracle; it reflects a transformed consciousness that allows her to match him at his own density."

Cynthia Bourgeault, The Meaning of Mary Magdalene

Pagan/Earth-based

"The heart of the understanding of death is the insight that birth, growth, death and rebirth are a cycle that forms the underlying order of the universe. We can see the cycle manifest around us in every aspect of the natural world, from the decay of falling leaves that feed the roots of growing plants, to the moons waning and waxing. Hard as it is for us to die, or to accept the death of someone we love, we know that death is part of the natural process of life. Therefore, we can trust that death, like every other phase of life, offers us opportunities for growth in wisdom and love."

Starhawk, *The Pagan Book of Living and Dying*

Kalil Gibran

"For what is it to die but to stand naked in the wind and melt into the sun? And what is it to cease breathing but to free the breath from its restless tides, that it may rise and expand and seek God unencumbered?

Only when you drink from the river of silence shall you indeed sing. And when you have reached the mountaintop, then you shall begin to climb. And when the Earth shall claim your limbs, then shall you truly dance."

Kalil Gibran, *The Prophet*

Death and Dying Experts

"The experience of the dying frequently includes glimpses of another world and those waiting in it. Although they provide few details, dying people speak with awe and wonder of the peace and beauty they see in this other place. They tell us of talking with, or sensing the presence of, people whom we cannot see—perhaps people they have known and loved. They know often without being told, that they are dying, and may even tell us when their deaths will occur"

Maggie Callanan and Patricia Kelley, *Final Gifts*

"Some common, clear lessons come to us from those who have been technically dead but were brought back to life. First, they share that they are no longer afraid of death. Secondly, they say they now know that death is only the shedding of a physical body, no different from taking off a suit of clothes one no longer needs. Third, they remember having a profound feeling of wholeness in death, feeling connected to everything and everyone, and experiencing no sense of loss. Lastly, they tell us that they were never alone, that someone was with them."

Elisabeth Kubler-Ross, *Life Lessons*

"Our Empirical experience of death is the disappearance from the physical plane of living beings. Such is the fact of our experience from without, that we have by means of our five senses. But the disappearance of such is not confined to the domain of outward experience of the senses. It is experienced also in the domain for the inner experience, that of consciousness. There, the images and representations disappear just as living beings do so for the experience of the senses. This is what we call 'forgetting.' And this forgetting extends each night to the totality of our memory, will and understanding — of a kind such that we forget ourselves entirely. This is what we call 'sleep.' For our whole experience (outer and inner) forgetting, sleep and death are three manifestations of the same thing — namely the 'thing' which effects disappearance. It is said that sleep is the younger brother of death.... Forgetting, sleep, and death are three manifestations — differing in degree — of a sole principle or force which effects the intellectual, psychic and physical phenomena."

Anonymous/Robert Powell, *Meditations on the Tarot*

"Death cannot be gone through from the outside, reproduced, as it were, in vitro. Each one of us must accept it absolutely alone, must and can meet death only once. The outsider, for example a doctor, can assist the dying person, can accompany him on the way of his agony, but cannot enter with him into his actual death."

Ladislaus Boros, SJ *The Mystery of Death*

Soul Remembering

"Birth and death are two sides of a swing door. To go beyond the gates of death is to gain access to the realm of the soul where you can put yourself back in touch with your life purpose and life gifts you may have chosen before you were born. Plato's haunting account of how souls choose their life paradigms, or life patterns, in the closing pages of his *Republic* was attributed to the insights of a soldier who had died and come back. Plato taught that things that are truly worth knowing come to us through anamnesis, or, 'remembering.'"

Robert Moss, *Dreamgates*

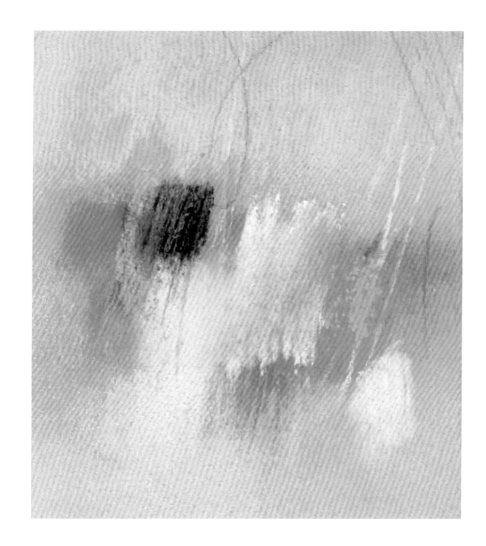

THINK ABOUT YOUR LEGACY

When we are young we believe we can do anything. We are convinced this life will never end. As we age, and mature, we begin to think more about death and dying — especially when we lose someone dear. If we are ill, we sometimes feel we are moving closer to the end of life. Many of us walk through life fearing death so intensely that we forget to live fully; we live instead in fear.

The best time to think about your death is not under duress but in times when you have time, literally, to mull things over.

In the following pages we encourage you to think about the legacy you hope to leave behind — for that will in many ways define the life you intend to live.

We guide you through a process that will help you discover your legacy and even outline your own funeral. This will give you something to feel proud of. It will also give your loved ones two less things to worry about: they will know how to eulogize how you lived and who you were and they will have instructions on how to truly celebrate your life as part of your remembrance service or funeral.

Define Your Legacy

Please answer these questions with your own heartfelt answers.

Who I am:

_____

_____

My most powerful personal quality:

_____

_____

What I stand for and believe in:

_____

_____

What is most important to me:

_____

_____

135

The people who touched me most in life:

_____

_____

How I will be remembered:

_____

_____

How I will look back on my life when I die:

_____

_____

My thoughts as I say goodbye to this life:

_____

_____

Now, if you join all your answers from these questions, you will have your legacy in one document.

136

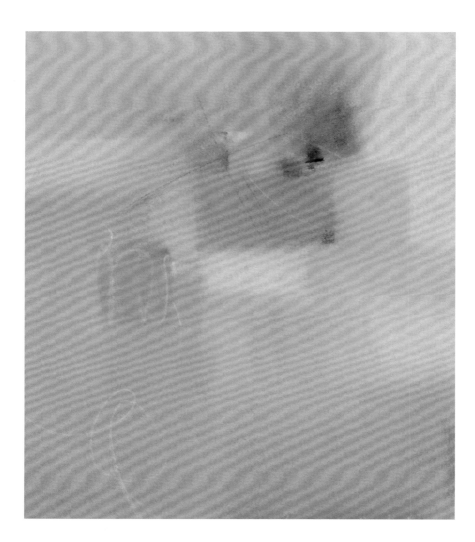

Planning A Meaningful Funeral

Many of us think we will never get to plan our own funeral or memorial service. But you can make some choices now about how you would like to celebrate your life then.

Here is a funeral or remembrance service checklist:
-Will it include religion or scripture, or intentionally leave it out?
-Will it be facilitated by a clergy person or a friend?
-What poem or reading would you like?
-Will there be music? What are your favorite songs?
-Who should give your eulogy or say a few words?
-Would you like to open it up for everyone to say a few words?
-Would you like to observe moments of silence?
-Will there be laughter and joy in remembering?
-Will there be a certain theme?

How will your funeral reflect who you are?

A funeral or memorial service seems a solemn affair in many cases, but it need not be. It can be conducted with love and joy. There can be happiness in memories, even if there are tears. It can reflect who you were and what you were about. And it can reflect your spirit.

Whether you are religious, spiritual or atheist, you can have a prayer at your funeral. Here is one of my favorites for those of you who don't believe we ever truly die:

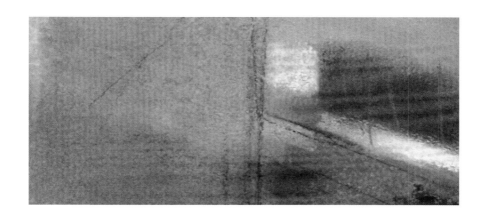

Do not stand at my grave and weep
I am not there; I do not sleep.
I am a thousand winds that blow,
I am the diamond glints on snow,
I am the sun on ripened grain,
I am the gentle autumn rain.
When you awaken in the morning's hush,
I am the swift, uplifting rush
Of quiet birds in circling flight.
I am the soft stars that shine at night.
Do not stand at my grave and cry,
I am not there; I did not die.

Mary Elizabeth Frye, 1932

Epilogue

Now that you've arrived at the end of this book, it's time to take stock of what we have read and see if we can come to any conclusions.

We've heard the opinions of almost 150 people, and there was a section on what some of the great religions think about death. Having done all of that, are we any closer to consensus? It seems not.

The majority opinion seems to be that death is some kind of transition from one stage to another. But there were plenty of other opinions, ranging from an agnostic "I just don't know," through deep religious beliefs, to describing death as a change in the vibration of strings. But let's examine the very idea of what it means to "know" something. Can we *know* anything, and how can we know that we are correct?

On at least two occasions I am familiar with (coincidentally separated by 100 years — 1900 and 2000), scientists believed, and announced to the world, "We are at the end of science. We know just about everything right now, and it is only a matter of taking our knowledge out to a few more decimal places."

An early example came primarily with Isaac Newton and the discipline of "classical physics." Isaac Newton was the first to be able to calculate the orbits of planets to a degree of accuracy unheard of before him. In fact he had to invent a whole new branch of mathematics, called calculus, to do it.

Famed mathematician and philosopher, René Descartes, believed those same ideas could be extended to the rest of science. *If only* we had enough data, we could predict anything and everything, and therefore there could be no free will — everything that happens *must* happen according to the inexorable laws of science.

This philosophy Descartes helped lay the groundwork for was called determinism. It ruled philosophy for hundreds of years, and still exerts tremendous influence over all of our lives, even though we may individually know nothing about the actual philosophy.

Classical physics came to its completion with Albert Einstein. Newton used the concept of gravity to master the orbits of planets, but he himself had no idea what gravity actually was and made no attempt whatsoever to define it.

That was left to Einstein, who explained it through two seminal papers on relativity (the special theory and the general theory). Einstein "completed" classical physics and that's when scientists made the announcement that they now "knew everything."

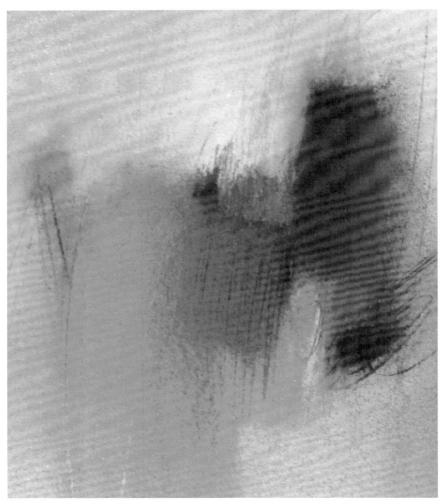

142

Science recognizes four forces in the universe: gravity, electromagnetism, the strong nuclear force and the weak nuclear force. Einstein spent the remainder of his life trying to unify the four forces – but went to his deathbed unable to do so.

Soon thereafter, however, other scientists took up the gauntlet and tried to come up with what they called "The Theory of Everything." Nobody was able to quite do it, but they came very close with a new theory called string theory (or sometimes superstring theory.) At that point, they announced once again that they were on the brink of "knowing all there is to know."

I guess I don't need to tell you that they were wrong! In fact, I find it amazing that they could ever have been so egotistical as to even dare to make such a statement.

We know that we are part of a vast universe of incomprehensible size. But up until the early 1920s we thought that the entire universe was comprised of our solar system. It was only after 1920 that we had powerful enough telescopes to see beyond our immediate neighborhood. Then we discovered that the earth and our entire solar system were but a tiny part of what we now call the Milky Way galaxy. Our sun is merely one medium-sized star in one of the arms of the pinwheel galaxy called the Milky Way, which contains more than a hundred billion stars.

And then in 1924, Edwin Hubble, working with the most powerful telescope on earth, discovered that there are an almost endless number of other galaxies. It is estimated that there are 100 billion galaxies with about a hundred billion stars in each of them.

In 1990, the Hubble Space Telescope was carried into orbit by a space shuttle. The Hubble has helped to resolve some long-standing problems in astronomy, as well as turning up results that required new theories to explain them.

So it's only been about 80 years that we have any idea how large the universe really is. And what do we know even about our own solar system? No human being has visited any of the other planets and we've only set foot on the moon. On our own earth, we know very little about what's in the ocean and we can't even *name* all the species on our very own planet.

We are making new discoveries almost daily. Now there's a theory called the multi-verse theory. Many scientists believe that our universe, as vast as it is, is only one of possibly billions of *other universes*. So does it really make sense to announce that "We are at the end of science, and know just about all there is to know?"

So if we *know* almost nothing about the physical world, should we be surprised that we know even less about the spiritual world, a world we can't see or measure with our scientific instruments or our senses?

We have a very good clue from science in the form of a theory called quantum mechanics. An integral part of the theory is called the theory of indeterminism, and is also known as "Heisenberg's Uncertainty Principle." The theory essentially says that *ultimately* we *can't* know everything there is to know, not even in theory. There is a basic mystery built into the fabric of the universe so that we can't predict much of anything with certainty.

I'm sure you've heard of the Serenity Prayer: "Grant to us the serenity of mind to accept that which cannot be changed, the courage to change that which can be changed, and the wisdom to know the one from the other." We can modify the prayer for our purposes to: "Grant us the serenity of mind to accept that over which we have no control, the courage to make the right decision when we do have a choice and the wisdom to know the one from the other."

So in light of the above, let's visit three basic questions:

1. Why do people die?
2. Is there life after death?
3. How can we handle the pain of loss?

Before I begin, let me say that I would *never* attempt to tell you what you should believe, especially in any kind of religious context. Only you can decide what rings true for you, but let's at least look at some different ways of seeing things to determine if there is anything helpful or comforting by doing so.

And while I have nothing to say about what you should believe spiritually, I do think that in a physical sense, science is a powerful tool that is not to be ignored completely. Of course, this itself is only a *personal* belief. There are literally millions of people who believe that the world is only about four thousand years old, and that God created *everything* one time only and that there is no such thing as evolution. I believe in evolution and God.

My personal beliefs have convinced me that, while science does not hold a patent on truth, nor is it any authority on spiritual matters, I can't ignore the basic evidence that the world is billions of years old, and that evolution is real.

Evolution, like any other branch of science, is hardly complete, and the theories are not infallible, but I can't ignore all of it because I don't believe some of it. The whole point of science is to propose theories and then to examine those theories though evidence and experimentation and thus to try to get closer and closer to the truth.

So now let's examine our three basic questions.

One: Why Do People Die?
(Especially good people, or innocent young people)

Somehow, and I don't pretend to know exactly how, life appeared on our planet. Of course I don't only mean human life: there are more life forms on our planet than we can count or even name. There is good evidence that there might be some form of life (microbial or otherwise) on other planets or moons in our very own solar system.

The chances of life happening may seem extremely rare. We can't even make an estimate of the probabilities of life arising, but just for the sake of argument, let's say that they are one in a billion. But remember that we have 100 billion stars in our own galaxy and over a hundred billion other galaxies that we know of. So the chances that there is life *somewhere* else, seem pretty strong to me. I am not so egocentric to say that I think humans are the pride of the universe. They may well be, but I think the jury is out, to say the least.

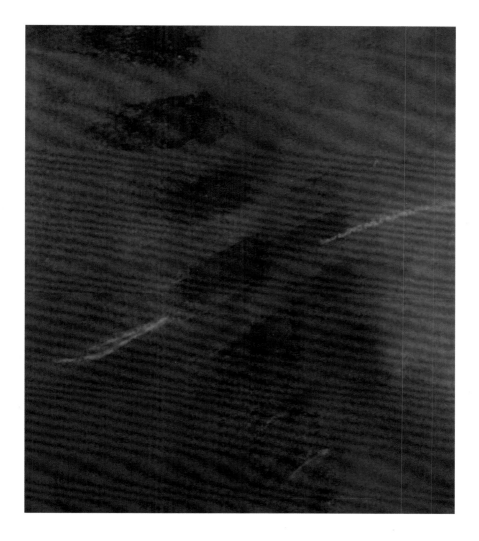

I don't pretend to have all the answers, but some things seem clear to me, at least at is applies to life on earth. Somehow life appeared, and there seem to be certain properties associated with it. It appears that all forms of life have a built-in mandate to stay alive and to pass that life on through some form of procreation. Any one individual might not live forever, but we try to live long enough to at least pass on life so that our species or life as a whole does not perish entirely.

This mandate of self-preservation is an extremely powerful force. We constantly talk about "saving the planet," but the truth is that our planet is amazingly capable of taking care of itself. We have been through an amazing number of "catastrophes." We've been hit by many asteroids and other bodies, including at least one big planet, which have at times stamped out most of the life on earth, and even tilted us on our axis. Yet, not only has our planet persevered, but it has become arguably better. Had dinosaurs not been exterminated, other forms of life, including ourselves, could never have come into existence.

Had our planet not been hit by another big planet, we would have no moon and could not exist. Had our earth not been tilted on its axis, we would not have any seasons.

Our planet has been through climate changes that make the current idea of global warming like comparing a firecracker to a trillion-ton atomic bomb. At one point our climate was so cold that we had what science calls "snowball earth" because the earth was so covered in ice that it looked like a giant snowball. Scientists estimated that no life could have lived on the surface of the earth during this period. And yet, apparently microbial life continued to live on beneath the surface of the earth and made possible many of the things that were *necessary* to our very existence.

In short we don't really know what is actually a catastrophe and what isn't. Without a very large number of "catastrophes," none of us would be here.

And while evolution seems to favor life, I see no evidence that it favors any particular form of life. No matter how conscientious we may try to be, thousands of species go extinct every year.

What we very certainly know, and it is reflected in many of the opinions expressed throughout this book, is that death is an integral part of life. If any species became immortal, they would soon overtake the earth and cause the death of every other species. In short order they would kill off themselves, too, as the earth cannot provide for an infinite number of any kind of being. So death is necessary for life in general to continue.

And we can die for all sorts of reasons. First, there are the physical laws of nature. Defy gravity and jump off the Empire State Building and you will die. Eat poorly or introduce toxic things into your system and you greatly increase the chances that you will die sooner than if you hadn't. Or simply live too long and you will eventually die. There are many things you have no control over, like simply living more than 150 years, for example, and there are also many things you do have control over: what you eat, what your morals are, how loving and conscious you choose to become, as well as countless other things that make you a direct participant in your lifespan.

The very inevitability of death is the most important lesson we can learn. If you know anything about the theory of yin and yang, you know that all things come in pairs, and we only know things by comparing and contrasting them to their opposite. How could you know hot, if you have no experience of cold? I could say that for any pair:

You only know	Because of
Light	Darkness
Happiness	Sadness
Good	Bad

And so on. Most importantly, life and death are just such an inseparable pair. We can't know one without the other. Whatever else you may believe, to me the obvious lesson is that you must cherish life. You must cherish those you love, because the day will inevitably come when they will die.

And it doesn't matter what your religious beliefs are. The main point is to realize how important your life is and to make the best of your life *now*.

If you take nothing else away from this book, I hope it's the lesson about how very precious life is, and you should honor that, both for yourself and others.

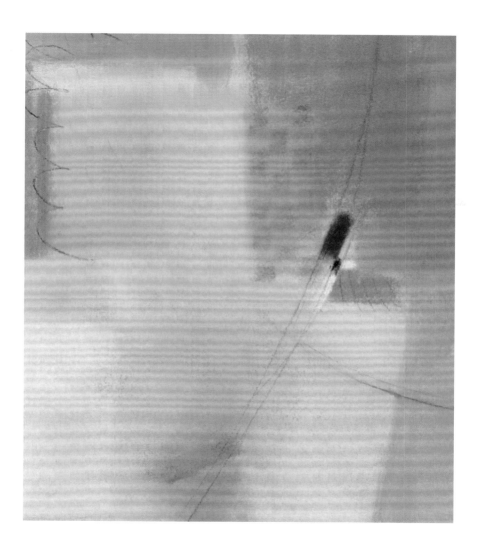

Two: Is There Life After Death?

There are two levels at which we can approach this question: the first is religious and the second is scientific.

Before we tackle anything religious, let's talk about religion in general. I happen to be an interfaith minister. Among other things, it means that I have studied many other religions besides the one I was born into. There are at least two reasons why I embarked on the study of other religions. First, I wanted to know as much as I could about God, and secondly, since I am the kind of person who is all about including everybody rather than subscribing to an "us vs. them" mentality, I was pretty sure I would be able to find things that all religions have in common, and that would show me the common ground where we all could meet.

And I must admit that I naively thought that all religions believe in some form of God, whether they called him Jesus, Jehovah, Allah, Yahweh, Mazda or any other name, seemed unimportant to me.

Imagine then how shocked I was to find that all religions do *not* believe in God. There are quite a number of them, Taoism and Buddhism being the first two that spring to my mind, that have no belief in any kind of God — no heaven or hell, no commandments or other rules to follow. So now, where was my common ground?

I pondered that for some time, and I concluded that what they all had in common was *belief*. In part, you are cured.

So for me, the hallmark of religion is belief. And belief, by its very nature is somewhat antithetical to proof. If you could prove what you believe in, it wouldn't be religion any more, it would be science. Faith, the cornerstone of any religion, requires you to believe in something for which you have no proof, but must simply accept *on faith*.

Because of that, I can't make any convincing and irrefutable argument for any religious belief about life after death. I can't prove there is a heaven. I can't prove there is reincarnation. I can't prove *any* belief, or we would no longer call it a belief.

Moreover, your beliefs color what *you* will see. A Christian doesn't see Allah when he or she has a vision, any more than a Muslim sees Jesus. So a Christian may see Jesus and heaven after death, a Buddhist may see the *bardos*, and so on. Each religion has their own idea about what happens and I propose that by the very definition of religion and faith, we can *never* make an irrefutable argument for any religion's particular belief. If you are blessed enough to be a person of faith, nothing I can say will convince you otherwise, anyway, so I won't even go there.

And diverse religions have some fascinating theories about death and life after death.

For example, many religions say that there is *only one thing* and that thing is God. If you make something, you make it *out* of something. If you are the only thing there is, then you make it out of yourself. So Christians would say that you are made "in the image of God." But Asian religions would actually argue that we *are* God. And since God never dies, there is no real death.

Humans (and all life forms) are made of things that we also find in inanimate objects. But *something* animates that pile of chemicals and makes it alive. For most religions, that something is their version of God — whatever you want to call it — and that which animates never dies.

Let's resort then to science. Surprisingly, we may find that science itself can give you more ammunition for what you already believe.

There aren't too many "laws of science" — they are usually classified as "theories." But one of the things that comes closest to a "law" is the "law of the conservation of matter and energy." It says that matter and energy can neither be created or destroyed, it can only change form. In more modern times, we believe essentially that there is only energy, and that what we call matter is really frozen energy.

But however we phrase it, the "law" tells that nothing really dies or goes away — it merely changes form. This is not something to "have faith in." It is one of the bedrock principles of science, and you have no doubt noticed that several of our contributors brought up this very point. So we know that nature isn't exactly creating any new atoms or elements, and that what we have is all there is and it merely changes from one form to another.

We also know from the science of evolution that life in general continues. All the leaves on a tree might "die" in the fall, but new leaves will come back next spring.

But of course, what we really want to know is what exactly happens to mom and dad or Uncle Mel.

Well, think about it (and all you need here is common sense, not even science). My mom and dad are both deceased, but I carry half of my genes from mom and half from dad — so they live on in me *literally*. But it isn't only their genes that live on in me; the very core of my being, the *ethics* that guide my life, were in great part instilled by my parents. Every person I have ever met has left something behind in me that lives with me right to this very day. No one I've ever known will ever die as long as I live and can think of them and continue to love them.

Better still, I don't even have to have met them. I can pick up a book with the words of Aristotle, who died almost three thousand years ago, and he lives on through me and all the thousands of people who have been touched by his words.

How many artists continue to influence our world even though they have been dead for a very long time? Through their work, they are alive still in our world. And how much more so is this true for Jesus, Buddha, Mohammed and countless others who have changed the world and live on through their ideas?

Your faith may also make you believe that you will see them again in heaven or whatever you see as the next life. Your beliefs

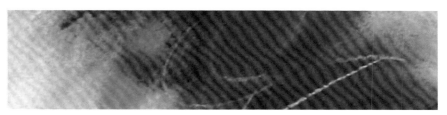

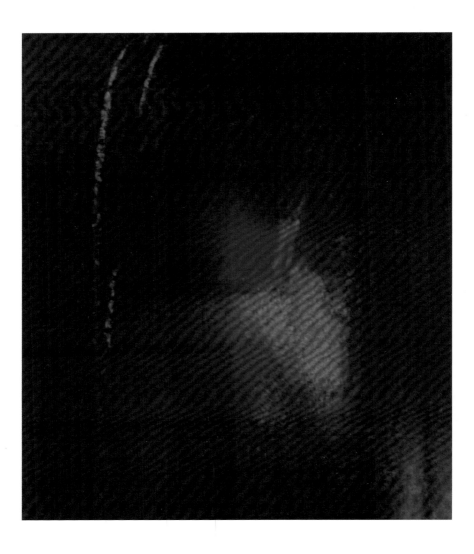

may enable you to "talk" to them any time you like and have them help you with life's trials and tribulations on a daily basis. But whether you believe all of that or none of that, you cannot deny that people live on in countless ways and that death is *not* the end of them. I do not believe we should dwell on death nor should we deny the fact that we will die someday. Therefore, we need to live each day with *love* in our hearts.

Of course, what death usually does mean is that you will never see that person in the flesh again, so you can't hug them and kiss them, for example. And that part is in large measure responsible for the severe sense of loss and pain that we feel when those we love die. That leads us to our final question:

Three: How Do We Handle the Pain of Loss?

Here, too, there are many possible answers to this question and most of them come, again, from religion. It may be comforting to believe that they don't really die and are waiting for us somewhere on "the other side."

I would never try to tell you what to believe nor to take away from you any belief that provides you with comfort. Like all things religious, they are, by definition, beyond proof.

And while we are on the subject of religion, it brings me to an interesting theory that Buddhists have. The Buddha was not himself a religious figure. He did not intend to start a religion, to think of himself as divine or to tell people about paradise. Although many people think that "Nirvana" is the Buddhist equivalent of paradise, nothing could be further from the truth. The word Nirvana means "extinguished" and the idea of Nirvana is that you will never again have to come back through reincarnation. You will simply be "extinguished" and cease to exist.

Buddha was shocked to find so much suffering in the world, and his only goal was to *stop the suffering*. Eventually he believed he solved the problem, and he encapsulated his goal in four simple ideas now known as the Four Noble Truths. (In a way, there are only three truths, as you'll see in a moment.)

The Four Noble Truths (simply) are:
1. **Noble Truth Number One**: All of life holds the possibility of suffering.
2. **Noble Truth Number Two**: Things have the power to cause suffering because of our attachment to them.
3. **Noble Truth Number Three**: Therefore, do not get attached!

Easier said than done. To this, Buddha answered with the fourth Noble Truth, which is often called the holy Eightfold Path, a guide to self-improvement that will lead to the end of the cycle of rebirth.
1. Right Understanding
2. Right Aspiration
3. Right Speech
4. Right Action
5. Right Livelihood
6. Right Effort
7. Right Mindfulness
8. Right Concentration

There are many people in my life whom I adore. I'm sure that is true for most of us. I've heard many times from people who tell me that their children and grandchildren are the biggest joy in their lives. I know a couple who have been together for almost 35 years, and they seem to love each other and respect each other more with each passing day.

But I also know that if either of those two people dies, the other will be devastated. I know that if one of those grandchildren dies, the grandparents will be devastated.

So what are they to do? Well, they could try to be unattached — to not care all that much in the first place. Or they can avoid such relationships all together.

But at what cost? Because of how sad I was when each of my parents died, do I wish I never had a mother and father I loved so much? Do those grandparents wish that they never had any grandchildren? Because I will be sad if my husband dies or one of my children, do I wish I had never fallen in love, or had any children?

I believe that for most people they would have rather had all that joy in their life, even at the cost of the pain at the end. I don't think they would rather have never fallen in love, never had children and never had grandchildren.

In summary, I would say these four things:

1. Life and death go together. To be born is to start on the path towards death. The only way not to die is not to be born. Therefore, know well that life is precious and fleeting, even if it lasts 150 years. Make every moment count, and love people *especially* while they are here. Don't wait for somebody's death to connect with them and treasure them.

2. Whatever else you may believe about life after death, in countless ways our loved ones never die. They live on in our hearts, they live on in our actions and they live on in

the hearts of every person they have ever touched.

3. The death of someone you love *will* be painful. That is a true measure of how much joy they brought into your life. The theory of yin and yang is inescapable. Every coin has two sides; the bigger the front, the bigger the back. The more the joy you have had, the more you will suffer loss. Only you can decide whether the joy is worth the pain.
4. Time and again, I keep returning to Love. Life is about how much we have loved. Love is the true religion of every soul.

And I leave you with my sincerest wishes that:

1. You realize how precious life is and treasure every moment of your life and of those you love.
2. You learn that love never dies and that often we can be closer to someone after they die than while they were physically present.
3. You strengthen your heart by the repeated exercise of loving and that you grow strong enough that you are willing to love completely even though you know how much you may suffer later by loss. For me, it is always better to have loved and lost than not to have loved at all.

With Love,

Lexie

LEXIE BROCKWAY POTAMKIN

Lexie Brockway Potamkin brings a diverse career and extensive world travel to her work as author of *What is Spirit?; What is Peace?; What is Love?*; and, now, *What is Death?*. A human rights activist, counselor and minister, she spent many years working in the world of business, entertainment and media. A former Miss World USA, she hosted her own talk show and eventually became a public relations professional working for Golin Harris Public Relations, Gold Mills, Inc., and Rogers and Cowan Public Relations. At the height of her business success, having founded and sold her own PR firm, she returned to school for her master's degree in applied psychology from the University of Santa Monica. Her ensuing counseling work inspired her to take the next spiritual step, becoming an ordained minister.

Lexie has traveled the world and over the past decade has been a guiding force and inspiration for many charitable organizations. She and her husband founded an elementary school in Fisher Island, Florida. Lexie serves on various non-profit boards, teaches meditation classes and she believes that giving and receiving are the same. The more you give, the more you receive.

Lexie is the mother of three children and writes inspirational books for adults.

DEBORAH LIEBERMAN FINE

Debbie showed early promise as an artist and was encouraged by friends, family and teachers to pursue her gift.

She was accepted at Carnegie Mellon, one of America's most prestigious art and design universities and studied there for three years. A change in her personal situation led to a move to Philadelphia, where she completed her fine arts degree at the Philadelphia College of Art.

It was then that life interrupted her artistic career. She took a brief 35-year hiatus during which she married, raised children and funded the family's life by creating and managing a three-store chain of award-winning children's furniture stores.

In 2007, with her son and daughter grown, Debbie decided to close her business and return to her art. She built a studio in her home and began studying with some of the most renowned artists in the Philadelphia area. Although much of her previous artwork had been in the representational style, she soon found herself drawn to new mediums and a new style — pastels, acrylics and abstract.

After such a prolonged absence, her return to the easel

brought with it a revitalized creativity and an invigorating burst of energy. She now paints daily — often beginning shortly after dawn and then noting with surprise how quickly the sun has set.

For some time, the excitement of being a full time artist was a sufficient end unto itself. But it was not long before the work demanded exposure. In short order, her pieces began appearing and winning prizes at art shows, museums and galleries. Although at first reluctant to part with them, she was persuaded to sell some of her work, which now hangs in private collections.

She lives and paints in Philadelphia and is represented by Emily Harmatz, who can be contacted at Emily@justtheright-piece.com. Debbie's website is dliebermanfine.com.

Final Thoughts

This section is for you, so that you may write your own thoughts about death and how you visualize your memorial or funeral service. You may find that writing your own obituary is a healing exercise.

Through this book I hope you can find more meaning in your life by contemplating, better understanding and accepting our inevitable transition into the next realm.

_____

_____

_____

_____

_____

_____

INSPIRATIONAL SOURCES

The Meaning of Mary Magdalene, by Cynthia Bourgeault

Silence, by Robert Sardello

The Mystery of Death, by Ladislau Boros

Christophany, by Raimon Panikkar

The Naked Now, by Richard Rohr

God at the Speed of Light, by T. Lee Baumann

Life After Death, the Evidence, by Dinesh D'Souza

The 5th Miracle: The Search for the Origin and Meaning of Life,
by Paul Davies

God and the New Physics, by Paul Davies

Wiki.answers: *How is a rainbow made?*

Newton to Einstein: The Trail of Light: An Excursion to the
Wave-Particle Duality and the Special Theory of Relativity,
by Ralph Baierlein

On Life after Death, by Elizabeth Kubler-Ross and Carolyn Myss

Spiriitual Aspects of Death and Dying, by Alan C. Mermann, M.D.

The Naturalness of Dying, Jack D. McCue, M.D., JAMA. 1995; 273(13):1039-1043

The Collected Essays of Arthur Schopenhauer, by Arthur Schopenhauer

Plato Complete Works, by Plato, John M. Cooper, and D.S. Hutchinson

Mystical Hope: Trusting in the Mercy of God, by Cynthia Bourgeault

Love is Stronger than Death, by Cynthia Bourgeault

Horizons of the Sacred: Mexican Tradition in U.S. Catholicism, by Timothy Matovina and Gary Riebe-Estrella

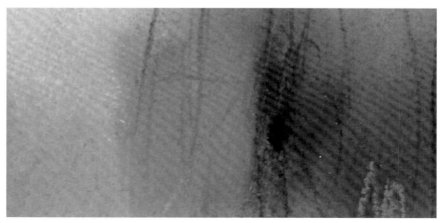

INDEX

A

Algarin, Rev. Raquel *98*

Allen, Woody *45*

Anderson, Gregg *127*

Andrews, Karen *60*

Aniballi, Marc *76*

Anonymous *49*

Ardinger, Barbara *12*

Asandra *8*

Ash, Tobi *112*

B

Bell, Bill *17*

Ben-Hamoo, Shlomo *42*

Benner, Gina *44*

Bishop, Kathy *68*

Bledsoe, Kenneth W. *60*

Boros, Ladislaus *132*

Bourgeault, Cynthia *107, 128*

Bredak, Andrea-Noemi *7*

Breedlove, Anna *3*

Britton, Patti *94*

Brockway, Laurie Sue *54*

Bruce, Robert *100*

Bulos, Sue *106*

Burleigh, Debra *23*

C

Callanan, Maggie *130*

Campbell, Joseph . . . .*i*

Canham, William *110*

Chappell, Lisa *72*

Christine *18*

Clark, Atonya *8*

Collins, Carolie 18

Colon, Dee 34

D

Dalai Lama 123

Dart, Hailey 44

Dini, Barbara 11

Dubitsky, Sorah 106

E

Edan, Michael 82

Elozory, Ra'anan 100

F

Farrell, Belinda 16

Friend, Deborah 28

Frost, Claire Noelle 21

Fraser, Trish 31

Frye, Mary Elizabeth 139

G

Gantt, Tamara Miles 115

Garcia, Kyle 39

Gibran, Kalil . . . . .vi, 129

Goetke, Randi 97

Gold, Jay 38

Graham, Sherry A. 101

Greene, Patsy 98

Guelbenzu-Davis, Ileana 49

Gunning, Stephanie 104

Guzman, Terri Giesken 114

H

Hardy, Kristal 63

Harley, Hilary 49

Hayden, Beverly 37

Henes, Mama Donna 74

Henly, Shirley 27

Henry, Jolee 52

Herron, Jane 50

Hickman, Pat 64

Hill, Michelle 119

Hill, Patricia 93

Hirst, Karen Lee 53

Hodes, Steven E. xi

Hodge, David 24

Hoeffel, Maryjude 120

Holeman, Jody 52

Holland, Henry Scott 46
Hudak, Mary Regina 80
Hull, Luann Robinson 72
Hundley, Mark 86

J

Jacobson, Rabbi Simon 126
James, William 103
Jennifer 62
Jensen, Dave 119
Jensen, Dee 32
Jones, Debra 31
Jones, Denise 34
Judge, Crystal 30
Jung, Lisa Kane 61

K

Kalogris, Lis 67
Katie, Byron 119
Kaye, Walter Ian 116
Kazlev, M. Alan 124
Kelley, Patricia 130
Kircher, Barbara 10
Klein, Clara 21

Kline, Kymberly 66
Krest, TJ 108
Kubler-Ross, Elisabeth 131
Kuriansky, Judy 54
Kyzer, Carlyle 14

L

Lavis, Kelly G. 67
Lee, David 22
Lee, Karen 57
Leghorn, J. P. 43
Leib, Arlene 2
Levin, Adrienne 1
Levine, Sandra 96
Lord, Hattie 47
Love, Beverly 18
Lynd-Hurt, Sabrina 104
Lynn, Jenny 49

M

Maggie Callahan 129
McClain, Constance 20
Miller, Roberta 103
Mindell, Arnold 7

Mintz, Mendel 78

Moates, Kay 61

Mohanan, Mahesh 73

Moore, Myreah Mia 90

Moss, Robert 132

Murphree, Debra Olguin 32

O

Owen, Barbara 13

P

Papier, Lee W. 69

Pederson, Lori 71

Persiko, Bo 16

Phillips, Marla 76

Pitts, Orion 93

Popper, Merna 98

Porte, Meredith 71

Powell, Robert 131

R

Raymond, Mary Beth 64

Repo, Jennifer 58

Rodriguez, Sonya Nance 119

Ross, Gigi 40

S

Sai Maa Lakshmi Devi 123

Schuchts, Tara Elias 99

Schuon, Fithjof 126

Skolnick, Carol 15

Slotkin, John 52

Solomon, Lewis D. 125

Starhawk 129

Sussman, Moshe 92

T

Tafuri, Maria 86

Terlevich, Molly 92

Thau, Dorothy 38

Thau, Michael 77

Thrope, Jacqueline Rose 56

Tonyan, Joan 50

Tralins, Alan 4

Tralins, Sonya Maya 105

Trause, John J. 62

V

Valverde, Fernando J. 25
Villella, Dominick 36
Volk, Steve 90
Voltaire 114
Votaw, Melanie 88

W

Warren, Wendy 118
Weiner, Hal 45
Weinstein, Edie 39
Wiedinmyer, Donna L. 37

Y

Young, Steve 27

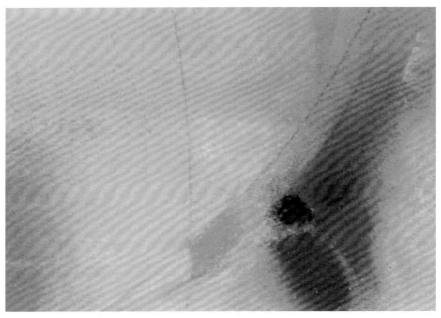